TODAY'S MORAL CRISIS ▪ "How can any American read about an 11-year-old buried with his teddy bear because he killed a 14-year-old and then another 14-year-old killed him and not have some sense of, my God, where has this country gone? How can we not decide that this is a moral crisis equal to segregation, equal to slavery? And how can we not insist that every day we take steps to do something?"

THE PROBLEM WITH WELFARE ▪ "For two generations we've lied to the poor in America and told them the government will be here soon. You don't have to go out and learn, for example, to show up on Monday. You don't have to learn to stay when you are in a fight with your girlfriend or your boyfriend. You don't have to learn to deal with customers when they are unhappy. You can avoid all this; let us send you a check."

HIS POLITICAL OPPONENTS ▪ "Now this is where it's at. This city is going to be a mean, tough, hard city, and everybody better understand that coming down the road. What you've got in this city is a simple principle. I am a genuine revolutionary; they are the genuine reactionaries. We are going to change their world; they will do anything to stop us. They will use any tool—-there is no grotesquerie, no distortion, no dishonesty too great for them to come after us."

WASHINGTON SPENDING ▪ "This is the only place in the world where you can increase spending massively and it counts as a cut. And it has been a major source of the problem of dealing with the deficit because you create a linguistic barrier to honesty."

HIS RELIGIOUS FAITH ▪ "You will have some left-wing reporter write a column about how can this hypocrite Gingrich talk about being religious. I'm saying this because what's happened is the left has established a standard of destroying people by discovering they're human. Anybody who speaks out then becomes a hunting ground for destruction. But that's not the point of this. The point of this is to say that since all of us sin, and since all of us fall short of the glory of God, all of us need to go to God in our own way and seek God's help."

FOCUSING ON SUCCESS ▪ "Where the people from the old order tended to hold hearings on victims and pain and failure so they could spend long periods of time studying how bad America was, we are going to bring in people who started at exactly the same place, but are students of how to rise, how to succeed, how to achieve, how to create. You're going to see a focus again and again on what is the solution."

HIS CONTROVERSIAL BOOK DEAL ▪ "I know there are important Democrats in this city who would have automatically turned down $4.5 million. They'd have said, 'I can make too much money in cattle futures.'"

THE STATE OF MODERN JOURNALISM ▪ "Now you have a devastatingly more cynical, devastatingly more adversarial system, which makes it harder to report the truth. Because the truth isn't always cynical. The truth is often romantic and wonderful. America is a great country with good people. And you're not allowed to report that because that would clearly not be cynical enough and you'd be laughed at in the newsroom."

HIS STYLE OF POLITICS ▪ "Do not shy away from controversy. This is a choice between two value systems, two power structures, and two visions of America. Conflict is inevitable and direct. Blunt debate is desirable."

HIS DEFINITION OF LEADERSHIP ■ "Real leadership is letting others invest their fears in your courage."

HIS RELATIONS WITH HOUSE DEMOCRATS ■ "The House is a place where for years liberal Democrats mugged Republicans randomly. The Republicans' job was to hand over their wallet and be grateful that was all they wanted. Now, we're sort of like the guy on the New York subway who shot back. We look confrontational because when we get mugged, we fight back."

TEENAGERS TODAY ■ "I think we made a huge mistake by creating adolescence as a zone where you're too old to be a child and too young to be an adult so you have this free-floating zone where the only thing that matters is peer pressure and peer response. I think it's crazy. It was a 19th-century bourgeois idea to keep the kids out of sweat shops, and it has absolutely got teenagers worrying too much about other teenagers and not worrying about being adults."

HIS CHILDHOOD ■ "I think I was very lonely and very driven. If you decide in your freshman year in high school that your job is to spend your lifetime trying to change the future of your people, you're probably fairly weird. I think I was pretty weird as a kid."

THE PLIGHT OF THE INNER CITY ■ "The evening news is a natural result of the welfare state. When you watch the killings, you watch the brutality, you watch the child abuse, my question would be: What did you think would happen when you put people in these kinds of settings and you deprive people of their unalienable rights and you deprive them of their God-given rights and you then say to them, 'Now you are less than a full person.'"

NEWT!

*Leader of the
Second American
Revolution*

DICK WILLIAMS

LONGSTREET PRESS
Marietta, Georgia

Published by
LONGSTREET PRESS, INC.
A subsidiary of Cox Newspapers,
A division of Cox Enterprises, Inc.
2140 Newmarket Parkway
Suite 118
Marietta, GA 30067

The author is grateful to the Progress & Freedom Foundation for permission
to print excerpts from the Newt Gingrich course, Renewing American
Civilization, taught in 1993 at Kennesaw State College and in 1994 and
1995 at Reinhardt College.

Printed in the United States of America

1st printing 1995

Library of Congress Catalog Card Number: 95-77268

ISBN 1-56352-226-8

This book was printed by Quebecor, Martinsburg, West Virginia.

Film preparation by Holland Graphics, Inc., Mableton, Georgia

Jacket design by Jill Dible
Book design and typesetting by Laura McDonald

CONTENTS

Few elected officials have come to high office with so much written and spoken on the record. Yet relatively few understand the thought and effort behind the memorable quotes and the 20-second sound bites. This study of Newt Gingrich will look at him through his words and his personal history. As reporter and then columnist, I've followed his progress and covered his career for 18 years; through the politician's defeats, his landslides and cliff-hangers, the investigations of his political ethics, the embarrassment of divorce, and the culmination of his life's ambition. My files show scores of interviews with Gingrich since 1978—in editorial board rooms, at political gatherings, and over a beer. For this book, Gingrich agreed to several extended interviews and was gracious with his time.

The reader of *Newt! Leader of the Second American Revolution* will learn not just the story of Gingrich's life and career but how his ideas and the particulars of the Contract With America were developed, and where his philosophy might lead the nation over time.

Behind each of Gingrich's well-publicized darts at the political establishment is an intellectual base that has been developing since he was in high school, collecting quotes and ideas on scraps of paper stored in shoeboxes. The reader is invited to see how the scribbled thoughts developed into a platform and strategy that ended 40 years of Democratic rule in the U.S. House of Representatives.

ACKNOWLEDGMENTS

The author should enumerate on this page the people without whom this work would not have been possible. But as Richard Nixon said, it would be wrong. The work would have been possible over time by anyone with an eye and an ear. Newt Gingrich has been talking and writing since he proposed a zoo for Harrisburg, Pennsylvania when he was 10 years old.

This work, however, would not have been completed in 1995 without the unfailing interest of the person known in my newspaper columns as "the lady who occasionally shares my name." My wife, Rebecca Chase, brought not only spousal concern but professional interest. She too has covered Newt Gingrich. Her beat for the American Agenda reports on World News Tonight for ABC News is social policy. Her expertise has been invaluable.

The people who brainstormed the project, Jim White and Chuck Perry of Longstreet Press, and Chris Riggall, my longtime colleague at the *Atlanta Journal* and *Constitution*, have been both patient when they meant it and subtle when their patience was feigned. My editor, Suzanne De Galan, has been forceful and understanding. She has the organizational skills of a cartographer.

My friends and longtime competitors, Frederick Allen and Don Farmer, supplied my daily levity. They and the colleagues on our weekly television broadcast offered the requisite humility lessons. My fellow basketball referees offered the "Newt Who's?" My phone friend and faithful reader, Dr. Howard Gordman, cheered me regularly. Two other friends, Katherine Cann and Jim Strong of Atlanta, proved to have better clippings than any journalistic pack rat.

Allan Lipsett, Newt Gingrich's press secretary, and Nancy Desmond, Gingrich's district director, were especially helpful, as was John McDowell of the Progress & Freedom Foundation. The Democrats trying to sink Gingrich on various ethics charges were patient with me in an effort to make their case coherent. I, in turn, have tried to present it evenhandedly, however much Tom Houck, my television colleague, might disagree.

Special credit goes to four people not directly involved in the project. The late Virginia Scott Miner, my ninth-grade English teacher, drummed home the basics. Donald D. Jones of the *Kansas City Star and Times* taught me respect for the language. Fred W. Friendly at Columbia University taught me journalism, and Jim Minter, the best-ever editor of the *Atlanta Journal* and *Constitution*, turned me loose on the printed page.

All that said, the project was driven by my daughters, five-year-old Chase and two-year-old Clare. Buy this book so they can attend Georgetown University or a lesser college of their choice.

THE IDEAS

"We must replace the welfare state with an opportunity society. The balanced budget is the right thing to do, but it doesn't, in my mind, have the moral urgency of coming to grips with what's happening to the poorest Americans."

CHAPTER 1

A
TWENTY-YEAR
QUEST

"It is impossible to maintain civilization with 12-year-olds having babies, 15-year-olds killing each other, 17-year-olds dying of AIDS, and 18-year-olds getting diplomas they can't even read. Yet that is precisely where three generations of Washington-dominated, centralized-government, welfare-state policies have carried us."

(from Newt Gingrich's campaign speech,
1993 and 1994; used also as a central theme of the
lecture series, Renewing American Civilization)

With those two sentences, refined from years of study and practice, Newton Leroy Gingrich found the message that convinced the nation to elect a Republican majority to Congress. That majority, seeing no one in opposition, chose him Speaker of the House, second in the line of succession to the presidency.

Those two sentences—one undeniable, the other contentious—are the essential Gingrich. He states unpleasant truths and confronts his foes with his chin. His stark words that ended 40 years of Democratic control of the House of Representatives are more than shock therapy or the product of polls, focus groups, and spin doctors. They are the end result of a career-long search by Gingrich for a message simple and powerful enough to convince Americans that the welfare state, born of the Great Depression, had been distorted beyond its original intent. A mammoth, overreaching federal government now is causing more harm than good.

For more than 20 years until that message was honed and repeated unto victory, Gingrich taught, debated, wrote, and spoke. From the time he was a young professor coveting a seat in Congress he looked for new ways to convey his ideas. (For some, his references seemed loony—from envisioning space colonies to praising the invention of the restaurant salad bar.) Indeed, the recent Gingrich successes are part of what he only half jokingly calls his "35-year model." The Speaker spent 15 years planning from high school on, five years running for Congress to win, 10 years as a backbencher devising ways to create a Republican majority, and five years as House Republican Whip, working to create that majority. By the time House Republican leader Robert Michel decided to retire in 1993, Gingrich's election to succeed him was a fait accompli.

In the afterglow of November '94, his election as Speaker was preordained. After all, a substantial number of Republican congressmen owed their election to Gingrich, who campaigned for 127 of them; supported them through his political action committee, GOPAC; and provided campaign and issue training for veterans and newcomers alike. Through the Contract With America, Gingrich offered candidates the goals and the language they could use to win.

CONTRACT WITH AMERICA ▪ Political parties, cobbling together ideas from hundreds of activists, construct platforms for their national conventions every four years. Gingrich essentially wrote his own, the Contract With America, a compilation of conservative Republican ideas molded into 10 pieces of legislation. The Contract, which included a constitutional amendment to balance the federal budget, a tax cut, a tough new crime bill, and limits on the terms of members of Congress, carried with it the promise that each of its items would be brought to a vote within the first 100 days of the 104th Congress. The politicians who signed it swore they would be accountable. In early 1995, the expanded book form of the Contract was riding near the top of the bestseller lists.

The Contract With America propelled the Republicans to victory and Gingrich into the Speaker's office, but it was, after all, just another political platform, even if it was a popular one that had been tested by polls and focus groups. The Contract by itself still would be gathering dust were it not for the Gingrich language that introduced it and the Gingrich political machine that marketed it through 230 winning Republican candidates. In 1994, Gingrich supplied not only the language of victory, he wrote the description of the problem, commissioned the solutions, recruited the candidates, and campaigned until hoarse for them. For the Republican candidate in need of support, Gingrich was hard to avoid.

In the television age, when political machines and parties were thought to be wounded mortally, Gingrich reinvented both. His weapons were as sophisticated as cable television niches and as hoary as self-help tapes for candidates driving down lonely lanes. The Republican political machine, which once pioneered computer mailings, phone banks, and targeted lists of likely voters, have now put on the menu talk radio, computer bulletin boards, and stopping places on the Internet. For the curious voter and those skeptical of the mainstream media, the Republican message was widely available.

In the campaign of 1994, Gingrich repeated the daily headlines, reinforcing what Americans heard and saw around them every day. His every speech on the Contract With America began by playing off the nightly news broadcasts, with their stories of child drug dealers, generations of teenaged mothers, police under siege, and public schools failing their pupils. He looked beyond the tragedy of the underclass, guns, and sexual practice to the social decay brought on by a system that had grown too bloated to react. The system, he said, caused those problems.

His words were blunt. Few among us like the truth in tragedy. And his two-sentence manifesto fueled the notion that the new Speaker was an uncaring pitbull who would turn the clock back to the 1950s. His message was clear, it was effective—but it came at a price. Mostly lost was the optimism that brought Newt to Congress in 1978, the sense of positive change, discovered only by the persistent who looked beyond the television news sound bite.

Politicians in the television age give "the speech." They stay "on message," which means repetition until the mind numbs. To the casual observer, Gingrich did much the same in the campaign of 1994. For the more committed voter who stayed for the lecture, there was much more to be learned. If the conservative press fawns over Gingrich, the mainstream press coverage of the Speaker, on the other hand, seems to be an unending search for hypocrisy or contradiction or changes in long-stated beliefs. But for those who have covered Gingrich for years and have the patience to study his views or read his lecture series, there is the knowledge that nothing has changed; the arguments only have been refined.

BARKING AT THE YELLOW DOGS ▪ As a kid, the adopted son of a career Army man—with all the dislocation that implies—young Newt was the one always a chapter ahead when classmates were called upon to read aloud. "Brains," as they once were known, had to talk their way into being popular. Any kid whose mother called him "Newtie" best be a good talker or quick with his fists. He had a startling change of ambition when he was a teenager. The would-be zoo director decided he would lead. He put aside a fascination for dinosaurs in favor of serious study of the levers of power.

Leadership took hold when the U.S. Army sent his father to Georgia. Newt was already a committed Republican when he entered high school in 1957 in Columbus, an industrial and agricultural hub for the central and western part of the state. Almost no Republicans existed in Georgia, and surely not in Columbus. The few who could be found were federally appointed postmasters and those few blacks who still owed allegiance to the party of Lincoln. In the Deep South at the time, even the very rich played Democrat, though they were beginning to vote Republican in presidential elections. "Yellow-dog Democrats," so named because they would vote for a yellow dog over a Republican, dominated Georgia politics. The real elections were the summer primaries when Democratic candidates were chosen. November was for football.

Georgians once knew Gingrich as a lone ranger. He ran twice for Congress in a district where Republican candidates were as rare as snow in a Georgia July. When finally he made it to Washington in 1978, he was for several years the only Republican in the state's delegation to the House. He came not from affluent Republican suburbs but from a district that included farmers who tilled the hard, red clay; a hefty concentration of union members; and middle-income suburbanites near Atlanta.

Georgians saw Gingrich constantly on the attack against his best-known constituent, Thomas B. Murphy, the Speaker of the Georgia House and the nation's longest-tenured legislative leader. Murphy was offended by a Republican representing the district in which he lived. Voters saw the young congressman pick fights at home and in Washington. One year, Gingrich recruited an opponent to run against the powerful Murphy in his west Georgia fiefdom. Murphy was unused to any opposition, and the campaign at home forced him to pay less attention to the state's other races.

Meanwhile, in Washington, Gingrich signaled a rebirth of confrontational politics when he took to television to attack powerful House leaders as arrogant and corrupt. If Georgians understood his methods, Washington did not. The political class wasn't prepared for the fury of his attacks on the federal version of Murphy, another product of the New Deal named Thomas P. "Tip" O'Neill. And they were shocked when in 1987 he began two years of assaults on the ethical behavior of O'Neill's successor as House Speaker, Jim Wright of Texas. Wright was forced to resign after the House Ethics Committee accused him of widespread rules violations. The upstart Republican called him "the most unethical Speaker of the 20th century."

By 1979, C-Span had come into being, bringing the proceedings of the House to cable television systems nationwide. When Newt and Rep. Robert Walker of Pennsylvania revolutionized the House by seizing on the television possibilities of the one-minute, special-orders speeches delivered to a near-empty chamber, Georgians again weren't surprised. Gingrich, after all, had been known at home to call a press conference to announce his luncheon menu. He avidly courted the media—he had to if he were to attract coverage in a state where Republicans were thought of as oddities who couldn't get a fourth for bridge. I first met him in 1976, when I was news director of an Atlanta television station. Years later, Newt could be found advising candidates in his training sessions to meet the news directors in their local communities. They are the media "nerve centers," he lectured.

Some eyebrows went up when Gingrich sought to run for a Republican leadership position in the House. In his home state, again, he seemed a loner, but that was because there were so few elected Republicans. Most ignored his bold mission statement in 1979, when he was a freshman congressman, that his aim was to build a Republican majority in the House of Representatives. Perhaps they had not read David Broder's 1980 book, *Changing of the Guard*, in which the prominent political writer said: "A Jack Kemp and a Newt Gingrich realize that the opposition party must struggle to achieve a cohesive program of its own, not only to test the wisdom of the government's policy, but to be prepared for its own return to power."

Those who were surprised by Gingrich's ambition also missed the behind-the-scenes activities of his 14-year tenure representing what was Georgia's Sixth Congressional District. (In 1992, when Georgia received an additional congressional seat because of population growth, Gingrich's district was switched to a safer, more Republican suburban area north of Atlanta.) In this Sixth District, Gingrich worried not just about his own campaigns, but those of other Republicans, as he recruited candidates for races up and down the ballot. The successes of those efforts dot west Georgia and the south metro area of Atlanta. In 1988, for instance, in counties where no Republican had ever won, the GOP elected 11 county commissioners, three legislators, two school superintendents, eight school board members, and a sheriff. One year, Douglas County, once the heart of good ol' boy country, even elected a black Republican school superintendent. Gingrich supported the candidates with position papers, fund-raising assistance, and his own appearances. The methods tested in small towns and counties were but a warm-up for 1994, when a similar unified campaign and training effort produced sweeping Republican victories.

SECOND IN LINE ■ Through all of that fame (notoriety to his foes), Gingrich wasn't known in the sense that we have come to know national leaders. Courtesy of our 24-month presidential campaigns every four years, the nation comes to know a dozen candidates intimately. The explosion of alternative information sources—tabloid to television news magazine—guarantees it. Ed Muskie's tears in 1968 in New Hampshire, Gary Hart's frolic with Donna Rice in the 1988 campaign, Michael Dukakis' ride in a tank in 1988—all become topics of conversation in coffee shops across America. Except for the loyal viewers of C-Span, however, the nation can't absorb the same detail and background on the men and women who lead the House or perform the heavy lifting in the Senate.

The ascension of Newt Gingrich may change that. He already is second in the line of succession to the presidency and could become a well-known national figure in the tradition of such House Speakers as Henry Clay and Joe Cannon, men who dominated their governments even as presidents came and went. If the Contract With America works and he isn't done in by his own words or the investigative efforts of his foes, Gingrich stands to join the Republican pantheon. For becoming the first Republican Speaker in 40 years, he deserves a chapter in the history books of the next century. How much space he gets in those texts will depend on his ability to consolidate his gains.

The Grand Old Party has its half of Mount Rushmore in Abraham Lincoln and Theodore Roosevelt—unchallenged figures. But in the modern era, Republicans are defined as much by losers as winners. President Eisenhower was a winner, but he brought no overarching principles to eight years in the White House. Barry Goldwater reinvented the conservative cause but lost dramatically in 1964. Richard Nixon, a tactical conservative who played on the strengths of both Eisenhower and Goldwater, was done in by his personal failings in the Watergate case. Ronald Reagan married the principles of Goldwater to the electoral success of Nixon. He reclaimed his party from the shame and stupidity of Watergate. George Bush was a transitional president, successful because of Reagan and his own doggedness, but defeated because he abandoned the principles of those who had gone before him.

Newt Gingrich is, for now, the successor to all—principled on policy, aware of the strengths and weaknesses of those who preceded him. Nothing in 1995 suggests that he should or could be elected president, but political movements are built by more than the people at the top of the ticket. Shifts in the political landscape come from ideas or calamity. That the nation now calls Gingrich "Mr. Speaker" arises from his planning and the failure of his foes.

EDUCATION IS FOREVER ▪ So what drives Newt Gingrich, this man America is just getting to know? Ego and the desire for power, matched with patriotism. Perhaps it is thus with most politicians. But Gingrich has an underlying philosophy that drives him to search for progress in the successful lessons of the past. He reinforces this philosophy with the discipline required of an academic. To him, words have meaning and education is forever. The historian in him demands voluminous reading. He preaches with enthusiasm about the need to consult biography if one is to learn how to do something. I was surprised to hear Gingrich entreat me to read Gore Vidal's *Lincoln*, a book the congressman believes is indispensable in describing perseverance in defeat and successful management of recalcitrant underlings. Few, indeed, are the conversations with him in which a book or two isn't recommended.

The Speaker is a jumble of contradictions. No one could be

more unlike the college history professor of stereotype. He dresses, for instance, not in tweeds, but in the all-purpose, year-round suits of the middle-management class. He can listen and he can be contemplative, but more often he is a blur of energy, motion, and what most of his enemies believe is anger. The hair is gray, to be sure, but the intensity of the man overwhelms the image of a kindly professor.

Professors, by tradition, are seen as cautious moderators of ideas. Gingrich uses language like a bludgeon ("12-year-olds having babies"; "15-year-olds killing each other"). He calls himself a "revolutionary centrist" yet has been called a bomb-thrower and demagogue. His carefully crafted lists of incendiary language, the words he urges his disciples to use, seem to belie his own centrist label—but only in the 1990s, when language has become homogenized, and political correctness saps truth from it. In historical terms, what Gingrich calls "contrasting words" for political foes are kind. He uses "destructive," "sick," and "pathetic." In Congress in the 19th century, disputes were settled with duels and canings. John Randolph of Virginia spoke of a foe "shining like a rotten mackerel in the moonlight."

Through the years, as Gingrich sought to hone and simplify his message, the historian gave way to the management guru and futurist. The three crafts entwine in the college course he has taught for the last three years, and the tapes and materials that have gone out to 9,600 candidates across the country. To Gingrich, the lessons of American history are paramount and American civilization is unique, not simply a shadow of European social democracies. He devotes as much attention to Peter Drucker's *The Effective Executive* as he does to the Founding Fathers and Lincoln. He quotes the confidence-builder of direct salesmen everywhere, Napoleon Hill (*Think and Grow Rich*). He can be Dale Carnegie and Norman Vincent Peale, but with a longer reading list. Newt is a futurist, lampooned occasionally for his advocacy a decade ago of vacations in space. Since he was chosen Speaker, academics have sniffed at his devotion to Alvin and Heidi Toffler, authors of such works as *The Third Wave*, which describes how the industrial age is giving way to the high-tech information age. This vision is essential to understanding the Speaker.

Gingrich organizes his life each day along the models of his intellectual heroes. Like Drucker, he tries to manage his day in 15-minute increments. From the legendary Alfred P. Sloan of General Motors and Gen. George C. Marshall, he maintains the priorities of "vision, strategy, projects, and tactics." Real change, he says, occurs at levels of vision and strategy. Vision must precede strategy, strategy precede projects, and projects precede tactics. Another Gingrich model is "listen, learn, help, and lead." In his earliest days as a conservative organizer among House Republicans, for instance, he let others chair the meetings so he could listen, absorb the thoughts of others, synthesize them, and arrive at a plan.

OPTIMISTIC CONSERVATIVES ▪ Gingrich's appetite for wide-ranging ideas—a sort of political version of "grazing" restaurants that specialize in light plates over sumptuous main courses—has led the intellectual class to dismiss him, despite his doctorate in European history from Tulane University. One Atlanta columnist was fond of using "loopy" to describe Gingrich's menu of interests and solutions. Even the Speaker himself is capable of recognizing his scattergun approach. "Maybe it's a nutty idea," he told the House Ways and Means Committee in January, 1995, after mentioning that all policy options needed to be up for discussion, including a tax credit for laptop computers for every inner-city child. "Let them eat laptops," replied the opinion writers. His keen interest in the sciences has led to his assault on the federal Food and Drug Administration and his insistence on new military doctrine, which he calls the "Cheap Hawk Solution."

His broad interests are a critical part of Gingrich's success. His willingness to look to the future and to trumpet change make him a compelling and tradition-shattering conservative. He credits former Rep. Jack Kemp of New York, not Reagan or Eisenhower, with doing more for the Republican Party than anyone else since Lincoln. Neither Kemp nor Gingrich relies on the conservative credo that what's past is prologue for what works or what happens. Gingrich relishes and encourages change and adapts past practice to it. Witness his Conservative Opportunity Society, made up of younger congressmen with a progressive, optimistic message, as a balance to traditional, prim Midwestern conservatism. In time, they saw their phrase adopted by Ronald Reagan, the most popular president of the modern era.

That word "opportunity" is as much a part of Gingrich as is Republican or conservative. For him, opportunity is a first job, whether it is flipping hamburgers or selling lemonade. In Gingrich's mind, the inner city—home to the nation's most distressing pathologies—is an opportunity for ideas to flourish.

His intellectual depth and the staying power of his ideas will be known to the nation soon enough.

Before that, though, Newt will have to withstand the fire of celebrity and political power. As he said in a memorable speech in his first month as Speaker, powerful forces are out to destroy him. It is not necessarily paranoia to believe that, when charges against him pile up at the House Ethics Committee with the frequency of new congressional resolutions.

The "Good Newt" is the Newt Gingrich of ideas and solutions. The "Bad Newt," as his enemies would have it, is the Gingrich of a powerful political action committee, a foundation dedicated to advancing his empire, and a college course cynically built to favor him and his contributors. That "Bad Newt" runs campaigns designed not simply to defeat, but to destroy his opponents. The Good Newt/Bad Newt conflict will go on for as long as he is in politics.

This book will explore what led to the making of this towering, controversial figure, how an Army brat born in Pennsylvania built a Republican redoubt in Georgia and reversed Sherman's march—heading north from Atlanta to seize the U.S. Capitol.

It is, to use a phrase he has adopted, a story of American exceptionalism.

CHAPTER 2

AMERICAN
EXCEPTIONALIST

"American Exceptionalism starts with the idea of a uniquely insistent and far-reaching individualism. It's a view of the individual person which gives unprecedented weight to his or her choices, interests, and claims.

I think this is at the core of the American ideal, at the core of the American sense of who we are. That we are uniquely individuals, and that each person is endowed by their Creator, every man, every woman, every child, is endowed by their Creator with inalienable rights. That's a very important concept. They cannot be alienated from you, they're yours, they're bound to you, and therefore, the system has to be built around your rights unless you voluntarily loan some of them to the state.

Notice the difference here. Because you have been given by God unalienable rights, only you can then loan them to the state. The Constitution says, "We, the people of the United States, in order to form a more perfect union." So we have voluntarily loaned to the government power. But notice how different that is from all historic experiences where the government, the king, or the dictator is empowered by God or by history in the Marxist model.

Now, Everett Carll Ladd outlines five key areas that he said were the key to what would happen: private property in the economic sphere, democracy and freedom from government control in the polity— meaning the political system, the political process— advancement on one's merits, the absence of rank, and moral equality in the larger society.

And if you think about those concepts and you look at what Ladd says in the chapter in Readings in Renewing American Civilization, *you begin to get a sense of how the vision of the founding fathers began to be translated into specifics.*

Let's start with private property in the economic sphere. Very radical notion for the 18th century. You own your house. This actually is an outgrowth of the Anglo-Saxon experience beginning with the Magna Carta.

We have a copy of the Magna Carta on display in the Capitol, on permanent display. In 1215, the barons said to King John, 'We will not allow you to raise taxes without our approval and you cannot have money to fight in France unless you sign this document.' Magna Carta means 'great charter.' And it is generally regarded as the beginning of the contract between king and non-king in which the king concedes that the non-king has power. 'You cannot take our money without our vote.'

Now, the barons frankly meant it for themselves. They didn't mean it for knights and they certainly didn't mean it for serfs and lowly people, but gradually over the following 700 years the concept has steadily expanded so now the poorest, the weakest, the most homeless of Americans has legal rights, legal powers, legal sanctions, and you can't have your property taken from you.

Jefferson started to write 'the pursuit of'—'life, liberty, and the pursuit of property.' The first draft said 'property.' He changed it to 'happiness,' but they thought, the founding fathers thought, property and happiness were inextricable. How could you have freedom if you couldn't own something?

And there's currently a rebirth of property rights around the country as a part of this reexplosion of the idea that you, the individual, have power against your government. That the government's powers are more limited than the individual's because the government's power derives from the individual. It also reflects the notion that the private market is more powerful than the bureaucracy, and that whenever possible, government should stay out of the way.

What they were saying, what the founding fathers were saying, was that we have the right of free speech. We have the right of worship. We have the right to be protected in every way. We can gather and organize a political party. We can do things.

Maybe even more radical was the concept of advancement on one's merits. There are several great books by Gordon Woods on the radical origins of the American Revolution that were very helpful to me in deciding to teach this course, because Woods makes the point that prior to the American Revolution, advancement was always a function of political corruption or of birth. You were born powerful or you were related to somebody who got you a job. You still see this in a lot of African societies where family connection is more important than merit.

One of the great struggles of our time: Do we really mean advancement on one's merits, which is Everett Carll Ladd's term, or do we mean group advancement? You deserve extra points because of your ethnic background, because of your sex, because of your origins? Which is it? Now, Ladd argues unequivocally the American tradition is that you are a unique individual. You are not bounded by your genetic code. You're not bounded by your past, and that every American should be dealt with as an individual and should advance based on their work, their merit. This is not a sense of IQ. I've known very smart people who were very dumb. I've known average people who worked hard who were better to have around than the smart people. And I've known people who were mentally a little bit slow, but their honesty and integrity and personality and decency made them more desirable than a lot of other people who were a lot smarter. So merit does not

*just mean some automatic take an IQ test and we'll rank
you. It is the sum totality of your being, but it's a very
important question.*

*It goes back to the core of being American. All
Americans are equal. All Americans have the same status.
And maybe I'm a little bit nutty in my populism, but I
think it's very important for us not to get carried away
with this idea that because somebody has a Ph.D. or a
law degree or gets appointed to some government job
they're suddenly fancier than anybody else and there's a
real struggle about, you know, how fancy should we be?
How simple should we be? And in general, I would argue
that in America, simpler is always better than fancy. And
populism is always better than being an establishment.*

*This is a society where the hierarchy is a function of
merit; it is not a function of rank. And there's a big
difference. The surgeon should ideally be the best person
to do the cutting. The commanding general ought to be
the best war fighter. It shouldn't be, you know, 'Fred's
son got to be commanding general. He lost a couple of
divisions, but gosh, he's a nice guy.' This idea of
advancement on merit, not on rank, not on who you are
but on what you can do.*

*Lastly, the sense of moral equality in the larger society.
The state can't make any of us more powerful, more
equal than everybody else. And this is a great fight in
America since about the mid '60s. Are we, in fact, going
to remain—now, remember again, this is an imperfect
society. The very people who were shaping this, as
Everett Carll Ladd admits, also had slavery. They were in
the process of transition. They saw themselves as moving
towards equality for everybody, but they didn't allow
women to vote.*

*I'm not describing some romantic myth, some Utopian
myth about a perfect world of the 1770s. I'm describing a
set of values which interestingly has more and more and
more become part of America. In fact, as Ladd himself
says, 'The essential distinguishing American values all*

reflect a pervasive underlying individualism.' In other words, you can almost see the last 200 years as a history of gradually, steadily spreading the right to be an individual to more and more people. The end of slavery and the gradual integration of the black community into the whole country. The rise of women as political equals. In the late 20th century, the sense that every person has a right to pursue happiness.

Whether you are mentally or physically challenged, whatever your background is, you have a right to be in the game, to be an American, and to pursue happiness."

(Newt Gingrich, from the Renewing American Civilization lectures, Reinhardt College, Waleska, Georgia, 1994)

Revolutionary, bomb-thrower. The words have become barnacles on a man who, in fact, is ever the professor. The incendiary image is so pervasive that readers of the comic strip "Doonesbury" now see the House Speaker portrayed as an old-fashioned anarchist's round bomb with lit fuse. The symbol joins Dan Quayle's feather and Bill Clinton's waffle in the strip's cast.

It has been popular to conjure up in just how many ways Newt Gingrich is like Bill Clinton. Superficially they share much. Both came of age around the same time—the '60s, the Vietnam era. Each owns a vintage '60s Mustang. Each admitted to smoking marijuana and neither served in the military. Each is an indefatigable politician who has come back from crushing defeat.

But if they have one certainty in common it is their educations and love for the endless discussions that are higher education. In Clinton's case, the love of dialogue translates into vacillation or compromise. Gingrich, on the other hand, prefers to listen and then to challenge and provoke. At the end of what to some is a meeting and to others a bull session, Gingrich has a four-point action plan, a scribbled chart, or a historical analogy. Clinton, it seems, is always the student.

Gingrich is either teacher or general. Clinton speaks of dialogue and plans. Gingrich speaks of vision, strategy, and tactics.

To understand Gingrich the politician, one must understand Gingrich the teacher and historian. For all of his descriptions of himself as a revolutionary or revolutionary centrist, he is better described as a counterrevolutionary. His goal is to dismantle the welfare state. If one believes Gingrich—that a unique American civilization took root after 1607 and flourished for 300 years until it was preempted by the welfare state—then the welfare state was its own revolution and Gingrich's is the counterattack.

His bachelor's degree from Emory University is in history and his doctorate from Tulane University is in European history, but we have come to know Gingrich more as a student and teacher of the American saga. His course, Renewing American Civilization, taught in 1993 at Kennesaw State College and in 1994 and 1995 at Reinhardt College in Waleska, both in his congressional district, seems more the culmination of Gingrich's academic work than does his narrow doctoral dissertation on education in the Belgian Congo. The lecture series has been criticized for superficiality, partisanship, and commercial plugs, among other sins, but it is a lively 20-hour statement of his beliefs, backed up by the Framers of the Constitution and his reading of history.

The lectures, excerpted throughout this book, are conversational, abetted by visual reinforcements in outline form and laced with video clips from the Cable News Network and other sources in order to make the professor's points. As befits a self-styled futurist, the lectures are available on video and audiotape and from on-line computer services. Discussion groups on the lecture series have sprung up on the Internet, placing the House Speaker in cyberspace, the place so many critics would like to ship him.

The intermingling of media illustrates why Gingrich is anything but a dry academic, why students in the 1970s flocked to his classes, and why he is more politician than professor. Few serious academics, to use a Gingrich example, would mention John Wayne in "The Sands of Iwo Jima" in the same lecture as James Thomas Flexner's biography of George Washington. Nor would the serious academic dare attempt an upper-level class that seeks to capture the whole of American civilization, much less offer the prescriptions for its renewal in the same 20 hours. Several disciplines take scores of bites of that academic apple in hundreds of courses around the nation.

S O L O N G , E U R O P E ▪ In his lecture asserting there is an American civilization and an American exceptionalism, Gingrich downplays the notion of Europe as the font of all knowledge. He joins Max Lerner, the great liberal columnist, and Everett Carll Ladd, head of the Roper Center for Public Opinion Research, in maintaining that American civilization is best seen as a *successor* to Western civilization. It is multi-racial, with many cultural traditions contributing to one culture.

"We're not western Europe," he asserts in his lectures. "We stand on the shoulders of western Europe, but we are quite different. We're more entrepreneurial. We are more open to people of all backgrounds. We're more future-oriented. We have no real class system. You know, in this country, the word 'Duke' may apply to either music or baseball, but it doesn't apply to a status of aristocracy. And so we're really quite different."

The belief that American civilization is unique is one distinction between today's self-made Republicans and the Eastern, silk-stocking Republicans, those old-money professional or baronial Republicans who inherited great wealth. Nelson Rockefeller was the break point for the party. He was the scion of American industrialists (or robber barons, take your pick). His education and lifestyle—Ivy League, mansions for all seasons—more resembled the English aristocracy than the three-bedroom homes of America's first-generation middle class, the ones voting Republican today.

Barry Goldwater's revolutionary campaign of 1964 began the break with the Republican image of the past. Richard

Nixon's 1968 intraparty triumph over Rockefeller confirmed it. Ronald Reagan's triumphant presidency cemented it. To borrow a phrase from the writer Mona Charen, it is the difference between Republicans of inheritance and those of conviction.

The party of the Cabots and the Lodges, the Rockefellers and the Scrantons, now is more apt to choose Hilton Head or Disney World for a vacation than London or Paris. Newt Gingrich, it would seem, is trying to codify the intellectual underpinnings of the shift.

DIVIDED BY THE '60S ▪ Gingrich argues that from the arrival of English-speaking people in Virginia in 1607 all the way until 1965, when Lyndon Johnson's Great Society greatly expanded the welfare state, America witnessed a long sweep of history that grew more positive and progressive each year. It is Gingrich's use of the year 1965 that stakes out the essential difference between him and President Clinton. Even though the Speaker of the House is but three years older than the president, they were on opposite sides of the great cultural divide marked by 1965. This divergence governed the way they lived and made for marked differences in how they responded to the military obligations of the time. By the time the draft became a problem for young men, Gingrich was married with a daughter, earning a deferment. Clinton left college at a time of higher draft calls and spent considerable energy avoiding conscription.

In *Destructive Generation, Second Thoughts About the '60s,* an insiders' look at the movement that expanded the welfare state, authors Peter Collier and David Horowitz date the cultural watershed to 1964 and the free speech movement at the University of California at Berkeley. Gingrich uses 1965. And 1965 was the year in which Newt was graduated from Emory University. Bill Clinton received his degree from Georgetown University in 1968, at a time of urban riots after the murder of Martin Luther King, Jr., and escalating protests against the Vietnam War.

The divisions among college graduates in 1965 and those in

1968—a scant three years—were remarkable. Georgetown University gave Pat Buchanan his degree in 1961. His traditional conservative views were shared by most of his peers. Only now do they sound harsh and angry to some listeners. Men of Georgetown's class of 1965 went willingly into officers' candidate school. Three years later, Clinton's classmates were more likely to protest, plot ways to avoid the draft, and test the motto, "Make Love, Not War."

Those who seek hypocrisy in Gingrich are quick to note that he led protests when he was a graduate student at Tulane University in 1968. But his protests were over the suppression of racy material in a student newspaper. He was arguing a constitutional point, even if his tactics were those of the counterculture he is quick to demean. Classmates of the time told interviewers that Gingrich was a 1950s sort of man, wearing a jacket and tie to class when dress codes everywhere were yielding to blue jeans and T-shirts.

For Gingrich, 1965 meant that almost 300 years of American exceptionalism were at risk.

"And what's been happening," he says in his lectures, "is that from 1965 to 1994, that America went off on the wrong track. Now that's an important distinction. There's a large block of intellectual thought that would argue America was really a sexist, racist, repressive, vicious society and we need government to correct the bad habits of the American people. Those people basically took power around 1965 and increasingly tried to redesign America....After 1965, the government and elite culture adopted ideas that are dramatically different from the traditions and principles of American civilization."

Gingrich, who as much as any politician has worked to make "liberal" an epithet, argues now that his criticism of the liberal reign until 1994 isn't so much ideological as it is pragmatic. Are the inner cities better off? Are our students better prepared? He waves his "four can'ts" as a banner, certain in his knowledge that American society can't survive 12-year-olds having babies and 15-year-olds killing each other.

As he says over and over: "These are not random observations by somebody who has an ax to grind. Go out and measure them and you tell me. Are more families broken down? Are more one-year-olds likely to suffer abuse? These are measurable, documentable facts."

POPULIST POLITICS ▪ For Republicans drawn to the party by Barry Goldwater and Richard Nixon, it may seem odd to place Newt Gingrich in the more populist wing of the party. After all, his first political notice came with his support in 1968 of Gov. Nelson Rockefeller of New York over the more plebeian Nixon. Gingrich then was in graduate school and maneuvered to make himself Louisiana chairman for Rockefeller. The New York governor's views on race relations and the environment played a large part in Gingrich's choice.

Rockefeller had compiled a strong record on the environment and was committed to the full extension of civil rights for blacks. To win in New York, Rockefeller had learned to practice the politics of inclusion. The racial issue was especially important to Gingrich after the assassination of Dr. Martin Luther King, Jr. Newt recalls that night in 1968, sitting up with his friend and fellow graduate student, Gary Davidson, an African-American, and together discussing their anguish. Gingrich, after all, grew up on military posts, the most integrated places in the U.S.—north or south.

Nixon, while offering Northerners a sound civil rights position in the form of his essay, "Building Bridges to Human Dignity," was at the same time formalizing the "Southern strategy" that caused many voters to read between the lines and see antipathy to black aspirations. Nixon was building on Barry Goldwater's breach of what was known as the "Solid South." But there was another reason for Gingrich's support of Rockefeller. The pragmatic graduate student didn't think Nixon could win the general election. He admitted as much to me in an interview for this book when I asked him how, in 1972, he went from opposition to Nixon to being state chairman for the CREEP, the committee to reelect Nixon.

Gingrich's support for the wealthy, liberal New Yorker in

1968 led to the first suggestions from critics that he shifted positions with the times or with the electorate. In fact, even as a youngster, he was attracted to Eisenhower in large part because the president believed in and used federal troops to support racial integration. Rockefeller's record in New York showed him to share that commitment and more. As for Rockefeller's history of generous state spending and zealous state regulation, Gingrich admits to a different view now.

"A lot of us in the late '60s and into the mid-'70s who thought that big government could work became totally disabused of that," he told me shortly after the '94 elections. "I'd had a lot more belief in the Rockefeller Reports and that whole vision of positive government, which in my judgment was the outcome of World War II. Then it didn't feel right in the mid to late '60s. And Goldwater felt more and more right. Drucker is brilliant in *The Age of Discontinuity*. He outlines why you can't do things through the state."

If Gingrich once was a liberal, as critics charge, it was relative. Listen, for instance, to the *Washington Post* on the Gingrich who won election to Congress in 1978:

"Just as the liberal Rockefeller Republican of 1968 had become the Nixon Republican of 1972, the congressman who told Atlanta reporters on the night of his 1978 election 'I am a moderate' was poised to become a thundering national voice of conservatism."

But of course Gingrich was moderate when one compares him to an opponent in his first two races: Jack Flynt, an old-school Southern segregationist. Simply by being in the South and favoring full integration and equal opportunity for all, Newt could fairly be called a moderate for his time. Because he was born in Pennsylvania and traveled the U.S. and Europe as an army brat, Newt never shared the age-old views of many Southerners on white supremacy and racial separation. He grew to understand minority status, first as one who shared his Army-post housing, school bus, and classrooms with African-Americans and then as a Republican in the heart of yellow-dog Democrat territory. But he never accepted it.

When he was just a year removed from high school, Newt

sought to broaden the tiny Republican base in Georgia beyond the monied precincts of Atlanta and a few other cities. He was a part-time executive director for the Georgia Republicans in 1962, helping to invent traveling party platform committees. He slept in the homes and farmhouses of Young Republicans and those few party officials who existed in Georgia.

Though he was the product of privileged education, Gingrich grew to understand that Southern populism was a natural fit with a conservative Republican philosophy. He also saw that the Scots-Irish stock of the Southern white was rooted in individualism, patriotism, and respect for family and church. It's not too great a leap to connect those travels with Gingrich's affinity for Alexis de Tocqueville's *Democracy in America*. In his acceptance speech upon taking the oath as Speaker of the House, Gingrich quoted Tocqueville's description of a U.S. House of Representatives made up of "vulgar" people. Americans, Gingrich notes, are fond of being called commoners. Lincoln was known as "the great commoner." To Professor Gingrich, the absence of class and rank is part of American exceptionalism.

Gingrich saw the same motivations and value systems in black Americans. He is fond of quoting a 1992 poll conducted in 10 Southern states by the *Atlanta Journal-Constitution*, which found that eighty-one percent of black respondents and 79 percent of white respondents agreed to the premise that work should be a requirement to qualify for welfare payments, even for women with young children.

SIGNS OF DEMOCRATIC DECLINE ■
Gingrich first came to my attention in 1976 in his second losing bid for Congress to Rep. Jack Flynt, a politician typical of the white-haired, slow-talking Southern Democrats known as the courthouse crowd or the Bourbons (for the land-owning class, not the whiskey of choice).

The young candidate with a flair for press attention was unlike any other Republican in Georgia. Most on the ballot that year were converts to the party, brought aboard by the excesses of Lyndon Johnson's Great Society and emboldened by Barry Goldwater's Southern sweep in 1964. Few were racists, but they didn't hestitate to tag Democrats as the party of George McGovern, Jane Fonda, and H. Rap Brown. The linkage was to their political advantage. On issues, they weren't unlike the conservative southern Democrats, as the nation soon would learn in 1981, when the Boll Weevil Caucus of Southern Democrats in Congress would vote consistently for President Reagan's tax cuts, for scaling back spending increases for social programs, and for increases in spending for defense.

As for the Democrats, even the mainstream stars were clouded. Sam Nunn of Georgia recalls that during his longshot campaign for the Senate in 1972, he often stopped along the roadside to take down McGovern for President signs. After McGovern and save for the false honeymoon with Jimmy Carter in 1976, the Southern Democrat was in decline and running scared for the center.

Even with Jimmy Carter sweeping his native Georgia in 1976, Gingrich ran well, winning 49 percent of the vote against Flynt. This was his second loss to Flynt, but Newt was becoming inevitable. It was an odd confrontation: Flynt distanced himself from his national party for its extreme positions on affirmative action and higher taxes and its weakness on foreign policy. Gingrich embraced views on race that would have doomed most candidates in majority-white districts. Already he was laying the seeds for the Republican outreach to African-Americans and other minorities that came to be when Gingrich met Jack Kemp and Vin Weber and helped create the Conservative Opportunity Society. While some Southern Republicans were making points by playing on racial animosity, Gingrich was following Jack Kemp in insisting on a bigger tent, with seatmates of many colors. He took pains to involve blacks in his campaign and worked closely with black churches in his district.

Southern Republicans long have carried racial baggage. It was inevitable when racial supremacists jumped on the Goldwater bandwagon and when Richard Nixon's campaign played on white anxieties. For young conservatives who believed in equal opportunity, party gatherings could be insensitive places. Gingrich always was different, pushing in every speech for inclusion and working with the zeal of a preacher to win over blacks who might be curious about his message.

His optimism comes first. "No other nation," he says, "has so successfully combined people of different races and nations within a single culture."

Jeff Dickerson, now an editorial columnist at the *Atlanta Journal*, recalls being amazed at finding an economic conservative in the South with race relations near the top of his agenda. Dickerson, a black conservative, wasn't alone. The most liberal editorial writers began to give the conservative devil his due, at least on the South's overarching issue. In some cases, early in Gingrich's political career, journalists dubbed him a liberal simply for the novelty of his positions.

A NATION OF IMMIGRANTS ▪ Gingrich's views on race were shaped by his rearing in the culture of the military meritocracy. "I was in an integrated society," he recalled in an interview in the spring of 1995. "I knew kids who were black. We formed friendships; we were in the same classes; we were on the same teams. We routinely interacted on a level where you didn't think about it. And they were Americans. In Europe the distinction was between us and not us. And they were us."

His views also are grounded in his historical view: *e pluribus unum*, or out of many, one. To use his phrase, "American civilization is diverse and multiethnic, but it is one civilization." Newt finds common ground with those who argue that in diversity there is strength—but only to a point. We are multiethnic, but we are not multicultural. He, like the historian Arthur Schlesinger, argues that multiculturalism only balkanizes us and threatens a society unique for its diversity.

At one time, Gingrich argued his position by insisting that American culture is better than its European predecessors. He could be scathing in decrying the racism of Western Civilization, the savagery of Aztec sacrifice, the oppression of women in Iran, and the mutilations of women in third-world societies. For a time, until the 1990s, he argued for "other-culturalism" on the grounds that multiculturalism is nothing more than "situation ethics applied to civilization." With "other-culturalism," on the other hand, students would learn of other civilizations within the framework of America's past. But the concept was replaced by "one civilization, diverse and multiethnic." He was making a decision on values. After all, he says, you can't have a civilization without judgment, "because that's how a civilization tells you what you should do."

By emphasizing the positive, Gingrich sidesteps the multicultural debates that poison so many college campuses. He proudly trumpets the United States as the first "world civilization," one that has empowered more people from more backgrounds to pursue happiness. He argues that each wave of immigrants enriches those who were here before. In his view, being an American is learned behavior. His lectures celebrate the immigrant experience in a way that civics and social studies courses in junior high school once did.

"I serve with a Congressman Jay Kim from Southern California who's a first-generation Korean-American," he says in his lecture series, "born in Korea and now lives here. I serve with J.C. Watts of Oklahoma [the black representative elected in 1994]. You may in fact be blended from a lot of different racial stocks. You may be Hispanic. I serve with Henry Bonilla from San Antonio, Texas. And yet each of them would describe themselves as an American. They know what they are descended from, they know their background. And, of course, if their children met at a congressional social event and married, then you'd start having to say, 'Well, I'm a European-Korean-American-African-American Hispanic.' It's easier to just say, 'I'm an American.'"

The nation, and in particular the South, has a sorry history of nativist thinking. That tradition is the reason alarms go off each time an anti-immigrant measure pops up. An example is California's Proposition 187, approved by voters in 1994, that would deny many benefits to illegal immigrants. People of good will (and the courts) still debate the merits of that measure, but put Gingrich squarely on the side of the legal immigrant. His indirect rebuke to the nativists is a clever one. He likes to point out that Olympic medal winner Kristi Yamaguchi and generals Colin Powell and John Shalikashvili are each American, without argument.

The immigrant success story has never sat well with many African-Americans, Colin Powell notwithstanding. It is fashionable for African-Americans to argue that forced immigration in the form of slavery hardly is comparable to immigration by those seeking new opportunities and the idea that is America. Gingrich rarely, if ever, confronts that anger head-on. Instead, he uses the lessons of history to argue that time and change heal wounds. The problems that so anger black Americans, he insists, came to be after 1965. It is a complicated argument, made more so by his choice of 1965—the year of the Voting Rights Act, the most important extension of freedom to a people enslaved first by law and then by Jim Crow law and custom. Still, in lectures and speeches he sticks to the sweep of history and the continual rollback of waves of prejudice:

"You can go back and you can take from 1607 until 1965 and you have certain long sweeps that are more and more positive. We go from slavery to segregation to integration. We go from empowering wealthy white males to eliminating the poll tax and then giving women the vote, then making sure everybody can vote. We go from almost the very beginning to acquire property. Free blacks as early as the 1740s and 1750s could acquire property not only in the North, but in New Orleans. And you actually had an entire class of people in New Orleans who were of African-American descent but who were free and owned property and businesses and could buy and sell and were part of the commercial environment."

Gingrich goes on to enumerate America's past hostility toward the Irish, Southern Europeans, and the Chinese. These immigrants' ability to overcome bigotry and succeed while so many black Americans languish is the prelude to the congressman's call for dismantling the welfare state.

AFFIRMING INDIVIDUALS ■ In 1995, one of those oceanic disturbances that characterize the political process washed onto the front pages and the newscasts: The issue is a proposal in California to place a referendum on the 1996 ballot eliminating affirmative action programs in state and local government. It is a bit early to tell if the sentiment to end affirmative action programs is a whitecap or a deeper wave with the potential to move governments. (As with so much that originates in California, the question must be asked whether the proposed referendum is a national trend or just trendy.)

By spring 1995, the major Republican presidential candidates had embraced the initiative, and the Clinton administration ordered a review of all federal policies. When Gingrich was asked about the issue at his regular daily press conference, he was consistent with the course he teaches each winter Saturday.

"It's my belief," he said, "that affirmative action programs, if done for individuals, are good, and if done by some group distinction, are bad. Because it is antithetical to the American dream to measure people by the genetic pattern of their great-grandmothers. So, I'm very interested in rewriting the affirmative action programs so that they allow individuals to get help whether they are Appalachian white or American Indians from a reservation or blacks from Atlanta or Hispanics from L.A...or Asians from San Francisco. But I think it ought to be based not on your belonging to a genetic pattern but on the fact that you individually have worked hard and are trying to rise and that you come out of a background of poverty and a background of cultural need."

A reporter pressed on, noting that some beneficiaries of government preferences have been subjected to discrimination for centuries.

"That's been true of virtually every American. The Anglo-Saxons were routinely discriminated against by the Normans, the Irish were discriminated against by the English. You know, go down the list. I'm suggesting to you that every group in American society—and I would say the Irish would tell you in terms of 'No Irish need apply,' and the kind of discrimination common in the 19th century—that was very tough. And it was a very, very severe discrimination. I think that Jews can give you a pretty good argument that certainly the history of Auschwitz is one which is horrendous, and we have a Holocaust Museum to remind people of just how horrendous it is.

"So if you start with what happened to your great-great-great grandparents and who you are, if you believe in integration and you actively believe in a society in which for example you may well have somebody whose background is Hispanic, African-American, European-American, and Asian, and that increasingly happens, do you then sit down and say, now on my next job application I think I'll pick the genetic code that has the highest probability of being admitted?"

Gingrich went on to note the problems of Asian-Americans in California who are being denied admittance to prestigious universities because of racial quotas. Note, however, that he didn't use the language common to the affirmative action debate for almost two decades. He didn't refer to reverse discrimination. He didn't use the word quota. Most striking, he didn't even use the word race.

The Speaker's comments were not carried on any of the network evening news broadcasts, nor were they reported in major newspapers. Newt didn't inflame the situation; he approached it from a new direction. That is exactly what he hopes to do to replace the welfare state and repair the inner cities.

CHAPTER 3

TWO VISIONS
OF AMERICA

"Let me suggest to you that the welfare state has failed because its core understanding of humans is wrong. Not because it doesn't have enough money. Not because the people who run it don't know what they're doing. Not because of some minor thing. At the heart of the welfare state is an error. And let me walk you through why I believe it's an error.

We said in our first great state document, the Declaration of Independence, 'We hold these truths to be self-evident: that all men are created equal and that they are endowed by their Creator with certain unalienable rights, among which are life, liberty, and the pursuit of happiness.'

Now, if you actually read that, not just as somebody who heard it for the 4,000th time because you've learned it since first grade, but you think about: What did the founding fathers mean when they wrote that?

First of all, they said it was so obvious, it was self-evident. They didn't argue. Secondly, they said: Power comes from the Creator. You know, the modern alternative might be for an atheist to say, 'Being randomly gathered protoplasm, we have rationally decided to give ourselves the following rights.'

A very different argument. The founding fathers, including Jefferson, who was a deist, all agreed that we are endowed by our Creator, so these rights come from God, not from the state.

Third, that they are very positive rights. Every person

— they said 'men,' which was an 18th-century term, but they meant men and women—every person is endowed with unalienable rights. These belong to you. And notice how positive they are: Life, liberty, and the pursuit of happiness.

Now, let's look at what the welfare state does.

The welfare state reduces citizens to clients, subordinates them to bureaucrats, and subjects them to rules that are anti-work, anti-family, anti-opportunity, and anti-property. Now, if you doubt this, one project might well be to go and apply for the system. Just spend two days being a person who's applying to get into the system.

Go talk to them. What are the rules you have to live under? Who will control your property if you live in public housing? What are the ground rules for living there? What will you get punished for? Under what terms will they kick you off?

There was a lady in Wisconsin who had scrimped and saved and saved $3,000 to put her child through college, but she was on welfare, so they forced her to give all $3,000 back. They said, 'Don't make your own clothing. Don't do the things that allow you to save. You're not allowed to save on welfare.'

Now, what values does that set? Go look at who runs public housing. It's not the people who live in it. It's bureaucrats. And in that context, I want to suggest to you that humans forced to suffer under such anti-human rules naturally develop pathologies. That the evening news is the natural result of the welfare state. That literally, when you watch the killings, you watch the brutality, you watch the child abuse, my question back would be: What did you think would happen when you put people in these kind of settings and you deprive people of their unalienable rights and you deprive them of their God-given rights and you then say to them, 'Now you are less than a full person.' So they begin to behave like less than a full person because they don't have a complete future.

In that setting, if you will accept that line of reasoning, efforts to reform the welfare state fail because they do not change the core values of the welfare state and because they try to prop up obsolete, dying, second-wave bureaucracies that simply don't work any longer.

Now, I think it's important to take those two and break them apart. The first part is that people, when they try to reform the welfare system, don't go deep enough into this first question. If you're truly endowed with these unalienable rights, what system do you have to live under? Because that would require you to rethink the core philosophy.

But there's a second part: Many of the institutions of government were invented in the industrial age. They were invented before computers, before telephones, before radio, before television. They were invented at a time when paper—you know, we wrote things out on paper, we filed it in a cabinet, and things moved at the pace of a clerk filling out a piece of paper.

Those institutions are all decaying because they're technically obsolete, and yet a great deal of our effort to prop up the welfare state involves not only the wrong philosophy, but it involves trying to figure out a way to make an obsolete system work. It would be as though I came in here and said, 'You're not allowed to drive your cars anymore, but we're going to provide all of you with horses and buggies, but they're going to be very modern buggies.'

And so I think we've got to rethink both the core philosophy of the welfare state and we've got to rethink the delivery system to modernize it, to say what does the information revolution give us in new abilities, in new powers and new opportunities?"

(Newt Gingrich, from the Renewing American Civilization lectures, Reinhardt College, Waleska, Georgia, 1994)

The idea of replacing the welfare state is so enormous most listeners don't realize that Gingrich is proposing it. But he he harps on it, directly and without apology. For Newt, no "reinventing" programs or tinkering with eligibility guidelines will do. His goal is not repair, but outright destruction, of the welfare state. The welfare provisions in the Contract With America—limiting the time a person can stay on welfare, eliminating cash grants to teenaged mothers, and handing many social programs to the states—are a first step in a long process.

Critics and commentators believe all this is an exaggeration. If their adult perspective was formed after 1965, replacing the welfare state is almost incomprehensible to them. The ferociousness of Democratic attacks on the Speaker of the House, the steady stream of ethics complaints and the daily personal attacks from the floor may have a simple explanation: Liberal Democrats know Gingrich is serious. And they must believe him capable of making good the promise he made in a speech in 1992:

"It is our goal to replace the welfare state," he said. "Not to reform it. Not to improve it. Not to modify it. To replace it. To go straight at the core structure and core values of the welfare state and replace them with a much more powerful, much more effective system."

The week after he became Speaker, he told Rebecca Chase of ABC News: "We are destroying children in the current system. When people say you're going to punish children, tell that to the four-year-old who was thrown off the balcony in Chicago and killed. Tell that to the seven-year-old who was raped in Cobb County by two 11-year-olds. The current welfare system is turning children into young animals and they are killing each other. There is a level of barbarism in this society we wouldn't have dreamed of when we were children."

Yet Gingrich has never embraced the view of sociologist and writer Charles Murray, author of the trailblazing 1984 book *Losing Ground*. In this work, Murray went so far as to argue that all welfare programs, save those for the aged, blind, and disabled, should be discontinued. But what would that do, Murray was asked, to the children currently living on AFDC, food stamps. school lunches, and the like? His response in an interview was halting.

"I think we would have to write off a generation or two of young people," he said sadly. "But then in some way we already are, aren't we?" A position so drastic is unthinkable for a politician. Gingrich prefers to seek ways to make most welfare unnecessary.

S E E D S   O F   R E B E L L I O N   ▪   After arriving in Washington in 1979, Gingrich had decided on two goals: replacing the welfare state and creating a Republican majority. The ritual advice for new Congressmen—go along to get along—is anathema to the Speaker, and he ignored the adage from the outset of his Washington career. In the early 1980s, Gingrich joined with congressmen Robert Walker, Vin Weber of Minnesota, and Connie Mack of Florida to form the Conservative Opportunity Society. The group sprang from an effort to spotlight the failings of the welfare state, even as most Americans were coming to take it for granted. The Conservative Opportunity Society also aimed to overcome the minority mindset of House Republicans, to challenge the Democrats instead of settling for handouts, and to redefine the language of political debate. It sought to replace the Republican message of austerity with an optimism about the future, a sense of possibilities to be unleashed by lower taxes and fewer regulations. In every speech, the young congressman talked of "replacing the welfare state with a conservative opportunity society." His language then wasn't as marketable as it is today. But it served as a dress rehearsal for what was to come.

(Reporters and opinion writers could count on Newt for these dress rehearsals of his latest cause or attempt to explain his revolution. I remember well a two-hour session on "iron triangles" and "new paradigms," the congressman expounding enthusiastically, the columnist nodding off. The academic in him could overwhelm the politician if he thought he had an interested listener. For nearly two years he carried his charts with him to every meeting. Gingrich's iron triangles were aimed at showing how bureaucrats, special-interest groups, and congressional committees frustrated the will of the electorate. Newt's pitch roused the interest of a few editorial boards and political scientists, but it didn't win big headlines and was shelved.)

The Conservative Opportunity Society gave voice to the young, aggressive Republican members of the House. Jack Kemp, while not a member, became the group's role model. Members subscribed to Kemp's ideas for outreach to minorities, removing barriers to business formation, cutting taxes, and "exporting the American idea." Kemp pounded home supply-side economics, world markets, and enterprise zones in the same way Gingrich hammers at history and the behavior of individuals. Each of those notions is a blow to business as usual in the welfare state.

COS members met weekly to brainstorm. They spoke the Reagan message of opportunity. And they said to colleagues: We are no longer comfortable in opposition. No longer do we nibble at the edges. No longer do we work on the margins. We have a message.

"The fact is that the Democratic majority makes proposals," Gingrich said in 1983 at a conference in Baltimore signaling the arrival of the COS. "They come in and say, 'Let's paint the room blue.' The hard-core part of the Republican Party says, 'No, let's not do anything. It's not the government's job to paint the room blue.' The moderate wing of the Republican Party says, 'Would you accept light blue?' The result is: Democrats always propose, the Republicans always divide, and one wing says absolutely not, and the other wing says, 'Well, let's just a little bit.' We end up being a penny-pinching negative party."

To Gingrich, Republicans were like the kid who went to buy flowers for a date. He wanted to buy roses but saw a special on petunias. He saved a few bucks, but he lost the girl.

T H E   E A R L Y   E F F O R T S   ■   Rereading Gingrich's

1984 book, *Window of Opportunity*, now is akin to reading a public figure's high-school essays. For instance, the congressman presented his ultimate goal in the form of a short chart:
"The basic changes I am proposing are simple:

From liberal	to conservative
From welfare	to opportunity
From the state	to the society at large"

Those subtle shadings are light-years from the Newt Gingrich who would destroy the welfare state and put the nation on a glidepath into the Third Wave information age. In 1984, Gingrich was discussing the "negative synergism of the welfare state." Newt had not yet discovered his voice; had not yet captured the quality of a Reagan, a Churchill, or an FDR to illustrate broad principles in simple language drawn from the experiences of the common man.

In *Window of Opportunity*, welfare programs received a scant three pages. Gingrich proposed that recipients receive cash and credit card vouchers directly in order to allow more choices and, not coincidentally, chip away at the bureaucracy. It was a precursor of the plank in the Contract With America to turn programs into block grants for the states.

In 1984, Gingrich said, "No one must fall beneath a certain level of poverty, even if we must give away food and money to keep that from happening." He urged the creation of day care centers for welfare mothers who would be forced to leave home to work or study.

But in another preview of the Contract With America, Gingrich suggested that minor girls should be ineligible for Aid to Families With Dependent Children if they became pregnant. Aid would go first to their parents or guardians. His language was softer then, more like an interoffice memo. There was no mention of orphanages or group homes, but the outlines of today's welfare debate were present.

A kinder, gentler Newt described this vision for public broadcasting: "We should involve public television and radio in bringing useful information to the poor, such as how to install cheap insulation, how to buy and cook good meals at low prices, how to take care of personal health and how to establish credit." Speaker Gingrich, of course, would kill the federal subsidy to the Corporation for Public Broadcasting, a small part of its budget, and force it to respond to the marketplace. Big Bird and Barney, cash cows both, would have to help subsidize the network that spawned their success. (When the public television lobby rallied to fight budget cuts in 1995, the adroit Gingrich taped public service announcements urging support for PBS—voluntary, from viewers, not compulsory, from the taxpayer.)

A SPACE CONDO NEAR MARS ▪ When Gingrich went to Congress in 1979, the Cold War lingered and President Reagan had yet to begin rebuilding the nation's defenses to bring down the Soviet empire. In his speeches and in *Window of Opportunity*, the congressman focused on the national defense, foreign policy, and the Strategic Defense Initiative ("Star Wars"). Ever the futurist, Gingrich co-founded the Congressional Space Caucus with Rep. Robert Walker, leading critics to dub him "the congressman from outer space." The Speaker's fascination with space and technology is related directly to his concerns over a permanent welfare state. For Newt, the welfare state drains budgets and stifles innovation.

In *Window of Opportunity*, Gingrich devoted considerable thought to expanding the space program and criticized the Nixon administration's failure to approve a space station program, with the aim of a colony on the moon. The optimistic Gingrich wrote of space with the unalloyed joy of a child.

"Imagine," he wrote, "that the National Security Council had understood that an America which aggressively moved ahead in space would overawe the Russians: The Russians would tread cautiously, ever unsure of what American technical secrets might be brought to bear on them should they indulge in military adventurism. Imagine that business and industrial leaders had been far-sighted enough to understand that a space industry would spin off earth-based jobs, using satellite antennas, new medicines, large surfaces and zero-gravity alloys. Finally, imagine a generation of educators who understood that young people need inspiration to motivate them to learn math and science, and that space was the adventure most likely to produce young Americans anxious to master these technical fields so essential to our survival."

He cited a 1975 study by Chase Econometrics asserting that an additional $1 billion a year spent for space would have led to 800,000 new American jobs. And he predicted the future:

"If we had developed at a reasonable pace from 1969, today we would have eight to twelve space shuttles, two manned space stations, and a permanently operating lunar base. Each news magazine would have a section devoted to the week's news from space."

What the young congressman and author got for his enthusiasms was a slew of nicknames and critical reviews of his book. Critics ignored the conservative agenda and lampooned him as a science-fiction fan who wanted to vacation on the moon. They couldn't know that a congressman who dreamed outrageous, impossible futures might someday control the House of Representatives, the place where all spending bills originate.

Those who question whether Newt Gingrich has been consistent in his approach to welfare issues should take note of his words in 1984 on what stymies space exploration and government seed money for biotechnology and futurist research:

"The amazing fact was that America literally stood on the Moon and watched in its living rooms as the dream of freedom reached out beyond our planet in 1969. And yet we turned back and wallowed in the problems of the welfare state for a decade. Food stamps crowded out space shuttles; energy assistance crowded out a solar-power-satellite project that would have provided energy for all; more bureaucracy in Health and Human Services shoved aside a permanently manned space station; the vision of a malaise-dominated decaying Western culture smothered the dream of a permanently manned station."

The bill for the Great Society's social programs now exceeds $5 trillion. Gingrich, it should be understood, is not like Ronald Reagan, who believed government is the problem, not the solution. Gingrich believes in a limited, but effective, government, especially a government that does what the private sector can't. He actively favors public investment in space and technology to prepare for the Third Wave information society. And he is not above hustling for appropriations for Georgia institutions, from Atlanta's Hartsfield International Airport to Lockheed's aircraft manufacturing plant in his home county. But it is his zeal to reduce what he considers nonessential government programs that caused him once to call Senate Marjority Leader Bob Dole "the tax collector for the welfare state."

WELFARE BABY BOOM ▪ How, then, did Gingrich move from the position of so many Republicans such as Dole—the welfare state, but cheaper—to his fierce belief in its abolition?

The mind-numbing nightmare of welfare statistics has had its impact on Newt's views. Consider a few statistics: The proportion of children receiving welfare who were born out of wedlock jumped from 27.9 percent in 1969 to 53.1 percent in 1992. In 1960, some 3 million people received benefits from welfare's main program, Aid to Families with Dependent Children. In 1995, there were 14 million people in the program—at a cost of $22.5 billion a year. From 1988 to 1995, welfare cases rose by 27 percent. The problems of the more than 5 million families on welfare are magnified at great cost to the rest of the nation. They contribute disproportionately to the costs of curtailing crime and drug abuse and to the difficulties of public schools—not to mention such large-budget items as housing, Medicaid, and food stamps.

But Gingrich's adamant belief in a better America without welfare goes beyond statistics to reflect the core of his political philosophy: Welfare undermines the strength of individuals. It is directly opposed to the notion of American exceptionalism.

In one of his lectures, Gingrich remembers a trip to Europe and his spin down the autobahn. He describes himself as a hapless American motorist doing 100 miles an hour, only to be passed by a Mercedes doing 160.

"But you know that tomorrow, if the Bundestag adopted 100 kilometers, or 62 miles an hour, as the speed limit, that virtually every German would obey it until the next election. They then would massacre the current generation of politicians and they would elect the 'No Speed Limit' party."

Gingrich goes on to note that for most Americans, on the other hand, speed limits are "benchmarks of opportunity," with the risks of exceeding them a calculated decision by each driver. *Americans, he believes, are not rule-dominated; they are incentive-dominated.* Because of this, today's welfare incentives are backwards in a democratic, entrepreneurial society.

His favorite example of how proper incentives might work with the underclass is a recent one, gleaned from his testimony before the House Ways and Means Committee days after he became Speaker. That was the session in which he thought out loud about providing laptop computers for the poor, an idea he admitted might be "nutty." As he exhorted the committee to explore new avenues and work to change attitudes and behavior, he cited the tax code's marriage penalty, or that part that affects lower-income citizens. Gingrich used the example of a man earning $11,000 a year who wanted to marry a woman earning the same amount. Because each taxpayer would be eligible for the Earned Income Tax Credit, a marriage ceremony and license would cost the couple $4,600 a year.

"And then you have politicians," Gingrich says, "who say, 'Gee, we have too many births out of wedlock.' And your government wants to encourage you to get married by taking from you 25 percent of your income?"

Gingrich doesn't blame individuals for socially damaging behavior. His target is the system that fosters it. He wants instead a system that guides citizens to the proper choices.

READ THE HANDBOOK ■ After almost 30 years of a welfare state driven by elites, notions such as perseverance and discipline sound almost quaint. Gingrich doesn't think so. Witness his use of the *Girl Scout Handbook*, written in 1913, to make a point. Gingrich, who prowls bookstores the way kids find the candy aisle, found the book in 1982 at the home of the Girl Scouts, the Juliette Gordon Low House in Savannah. Few politicians would find their opportunity society lurking in a volume most would believe to be a relic. Gingrich, on the other hand, says the book helped him decide that American social problems were more cultural than political.

"Choose a career," said the handbook. "Be prepared for what is going to happen to you in the future. If you're in a situation where you are earning money, think what you are going to do when you finish that job. You ought to be learning some proper trade to take up and save your pay in the meantime to keep you going until you get an employment in your new trade. And try to learn something of a second trade in case the first one fails you at any time, as so very often happens."

Gingrich recalls that six weeks after discovering this manual, a visiting delegation of unemployed steel workers came to see him, suggesting that Congress had an obligation to create jobs. He said to one them, "What if you have to learn a new job?"

The young man replied, "No, I've already picked my career. Now I've got my career and it's your job to make sure it works."

As Gingrich puts it, "The man's culture was telling him something that just isn't possible."

He contrasted it with the advice to young women almost a century ago.

"They were told that trades die. Professions disappear. They had seen the Second Wave evolution. The book fits the Toffler model. They'd seen the change from the agricultural to the industrial. They'd seen knitting at home, commercial knitting, cottage industries, wiped out by textile mills. They'd seen the changes and were prepared."

STARK CHOICES ▪ The issue of welfare is tied inextricably to the plight of the inner cities, where illegitimate births approach 70 percent and where even the most ardent liberals admit that generational poverty reigns. Unlike many politicians on the right, Gingrich's lifelong commitment to civil rights always drew him back to the problem of urban blight, even when he was representing Georgia's mostly rural Sixth Congressional District. His home in Carrollton was almost at the border with Alabama, a good hike from what most of us know as urban pathologies.

Since 1992, with his district redrawn to cover the north Atlanta suburbs, he is even further removed. His district is the most affluent in the state, and African-American voters make up only five percent of it. From this Republican bastion in Atlanta's most affluent suburban arc, Gingrich could sidestep those questions. But that never has been his style.

"We cannot shy away from controversy. I believe this is a choice between two value systems, two power structures, and two visions of America," he lectures in his most apocalyptic manner. "I think that conflict between them is inevitable and direct. Blunt debate is desirable. What I mean by that is that cultural poverty is devastating. Its costs are unbelievable. I'm prepared to say bluntly I don't think 12-year-olds ought to have children, period. I think we ought to adopt rules so that we minimize the likelihood of that happening. I think every person should work, period. Now, that's going to lead to a debate. I think that's fine. We need the debate."

That debate, for Gingrich, would be between the culture of poverty and the culture of opportunity.

In keeping with the notion of American exceptionalism, Gingrich has come to believe that the welfare state's greatest failing is that it directly and indirectly undermines the strength of individuals. Public policy should be asking how its efforts will help people become more responsible and productive and safer. Instead, believes the Speaker, the welfare state undermines discipline by discouraging work. It undermines the family by discouraging marriage through the tax code and welfare rules. Its rules and red tape undermine integrity.

If government changes its ways—or at least gets out of the way—individuals can savor one of the Gingrich maxims, "I didn't have any money, but I wasn't poor."

CHAPTER 4

CHANGING
THE CULTURE
OF POVERTY

"First of all, when I look at an inner city from the standpoint of saving the inner city, I see an asset. The people who are keeping the welfare state, they see a problem. I want to know: How do we liberate all those millions of poor people so they are productive, working citizens, so they are actively involved?

And I see every one of those folks as an asset we haven't been able to liberate rather than as a problem that we have to subsidize and support. Now, those are two very, very different ways of seeing human beings. I see them as a citizen and you'll see the differences.

Second, I want to focus on the inner city on strength. The welfare state focuses on weakness. So I want to find out: Tell me what your strengths are that we can build on. Tell me what you can do, and tomorrow we'll get you to do a little more. Tell me what you can do today, and let's work together and see if tomorrow you can do one percent more.

And recognize that it's a long journey. I mean, one of the things we do in the welfare state is we lie to the poor. We keep trying to find an easy way to be non-poor. Well, every person who's in this room represents several generations of human capital. Your grandmother invested in you. Your mother invested in you. Your grandmother had her grandmother invest in her. You have a long tradition of acculturating you to the work habit and the learning habit and the productivity habits that have allowed you to become a college student.

Now we find some poor person who's had no really deep investment in the capital in the human being, and we walk up to them and say, 'Hi. How would you like to catch up with somebody who represents three generations of effort?' You can't do that in an hour. And that's where the movie 'Trading Places,' which was a very funny movie, is totally wrong. It's crazy. You can't, in fact, swap places. And it cheats the poor to pretend you can, because people who have middle-class work habits, who are bourgeois, who are used to saving and used to working and used to doing all these things have an enormous difference in their approach.

Ask a very good friend of mine—we talked about this under "Personal Strength" and I read from his letter— Pat Rooney of Golden Rule Insurance, who joined a black church; he happens to be white, but he joined a black church almost 20 years ago because he wanted to be a fellow citizen and understand the problems of race in America. I think there are two white families in the about 1,000-member church in Indianapolis, and he made two points to me.

He said, first of all, virtually no one who's in that particular church is poor. Some people don't have a lot of money, but they have the work habits, the attitudes, the patterns, and their children are going to have a better future. And they're not poor in the sense we're describing in terms of public housing.

He said, second, from everything he can tell, the biggest single difference comes from an article he read in an IBM magazine over 20 years ago, and that's: How long is your time horizon? That middle-class people always focus on the future. And you might think about your own lives in that sense. They will not—they will always delay gratification for a better future.

And again, 'always' is too big a word. Nobody's perfect. Everybody goes occasionally for gratification. All of you have occasionally decided to do your test later, or as somebody said to me before we started this morning, stay up until 3:00 in the morning doing a paper that you should have done a week ago. That's just human nature.

But the pattern is that most days, most middle-class people will do things that pay off over time. Most genuinely poor people will do things that have an immediate payoff but then cost them the future. Whereas middle-class people are delaying the present to increase the future, genuinely poor people are wiping out the future in order to accommodate the present. It's a psychological, attitudinal, time problem.

It was characterized for me by a lady in Idaho who showed me a picture of herself and her brother on an unpainted family porch in the 1920s, who's now in her 70s, in a very rural northern mountain part of Idaho, and she said we had no money, but we were not poor. That our attitudes were all about the future, and we were, in fact, remarkably middle class but without income. So we couldn't afford to paint the house, but we knew all the values of work, of cleanliness, of saving, of studying. And she became ultimately a national committeewoman from Idaho who's quite a remarkable woman. And it struck me: That's exactly the right term. 'We had no money but we were not poor.'

It's a very important key distinction. So I look at the strengths of what you can do, not the weaknesses that we have to subsidize. Those of us who want to save the inner city see every person in the inner city as a citizen, fully empowered, fully strengthened. The welfare state sees them as a client, weak, helpless, a victim, somebody who can only survive if the bureaucracy takes care of them and nurtures them. Which leads me to make the distinction between our vision of them as a resource and the welfare state's vision of them as a victim.

Finally, I think because we see them as a resource and as a citizen, we believe there's a responsibility, where the welfare state looks for an excuse. So my answer would be if I went into a public housing project and saw people who were being subsidized, who didn't work, they got money from the government every day or every month, they had the money and they're sitting in a public housing project: We had given them a place to stay.

My first question to them would be: How far away is the library? I mean, explain to me why I should feel sympathy for you if you have 24 hours a day, seven days a week, nothing to do, and you cannot find the nearest public library.

If they say, 'Well, I don't have mass transit,' or, 'I don't know how to find the bus,' I, frankly, would laugh at them. I'd say, 'Then learn. There has to be a person in this project who has a telephone.' In fact, in projects now, almost everybody has a telephone. 'Look up "library" in the phone book. Call it. Ask them where they are.'

My point being this: You can't save people if you start with a presumption that they are beneath saving. I mean, the great destructiveness of the welfare state is it says to people: Let me give you another excuse not to be responsible for your own life, and then it subsidizes them."

(Newt Gingrich, from the Renewing American Civilization lectures, Reinhardt College, Waleska, Georgia, 1994)

Replacing the welfare state means building something in its place. When Newt Gingrich and his conservative colleagues turn toward the specifics of making inner cities safe and livable, a unified approach is shattered. Even for the Gingrich of "vision, strategy, projects, and tactics," the prospects are daunting. He searches to find ways to make people understand the opportunities before them.

He has no silver bullet, no magic wand. Newt comes at the welfare state debate from an unexpected direction. He doesn't blame people in the system; he blames the bureaucrats who run it and those who created it. Nor does he blame the absence of political will or dollars.

"It's not the absence of courage," he says, "It's the absence of sound ideas. We don't know what to spend the money on. We don't know how to structure the spending."

As with so many politicians before him, Gingrich proposes a series of pilot programs to see what works. His are at least different. And they are blunt. Gingrich wants to invent an entirely new system. Does he mean it? Increasingly, it seems so.

THE D.C. EXPERIMENT ▪ In the first 100 days of the 104th Congress, the House had little time to consider anything outside the Contract With America. It was forced, however, to confront the emergency cash shortage of the District of Columbia, which was scheduled to run out of funds in May. In April, 1995, President Clinton signed a bill to create a five-member control board to oversee the District of Columbia's finances. The bloated District payroll and the Calcutta-like squalor of so much of the nation's capital was seized as an opportunity by the Speaker. Gingrich and Jack Kemp, the former Secretary of Housing and Urban Development, are using the bill—which mandates the toughest financial controls ever imposed on any American city—as an opportunity to experiment with a broad series of reforms to end the culture of poverty. In the coming months, Kemp will work with D.C. Mayor Marion Barry on breaking with the past and trying new solutions.

In an interview after the House passed the measure, I asked Gingrich if Barry was agreeable to the scope of change the Republicans might try. "They're ready to try anything," he said. "The level of decay is so bad and the level of violence is so bad, they are terrified."

Gingrich's speeches and lectures from the last 20 years are full of descriptions of the kinds of reforms he would like to see take place in the capital.

In a speech in March, 1995, to business leaders in suburban Atlanta, Gingrich noted that the public school system in the District of Columbia spends $9,600 a year per pupil, nearly double the national average. He suggested that for such a high level of spending, each child could have private tutors and personal transportation to school—plus lunch. He advocates vouchers to parents so they can choose the schools, public or private, their children will attend.

"I think we ought to voucherize every program in the inner city," he says, "with cash payments to parents allowing them to decide where and what to purchase, be it an elementary school, health care, or groceries." Some in his audience thought he was exaggerating to make a point. In a later interview, he was willing to go even further. "Suppose you need to get children away from failed teachers," he suggested. "What if we called on the home-schoolers in Maryland and Virginia to come into D.C. for a massive home schooling program, teaching parents how to teach their children."

Newt also has suggested exempting Washington, D.C., residents from the federal income tax to encourage the productive, and he and Kemp are arguing for lower business taxes for firms that create city jobs. Kemp likens what can happen in the District of Columbia to what has happened to Hong Kong, a free trade zone where economic enterprise was encouraged and blossomed.

BOOT CAMP ▪ In at least three of his lectures, Gingrich touches on the culture of poverty and violence, or what liberals routinely call the culture of "hopelessness and despair." Now hopelessness has become blamelessness. Horatio Alger success stories served America well until recent years, when groups began to transcend individuals, and one's status as a member of a victimized group began to outweigh individual possibilities.

To use the language of Professor Gingrich: "The modern welfare state basically says to you: 'Tell us what kind of a victim you are and we'll tell you how big a check you get. In the American civilization model we study winners. In the elite culture model, we focus on losers." And put still another way, "Does your future matter and your effort matter, or does your past matter?"

The culture of poverty and violence is emotional to him. "I

take it personally," he said in a speech in his district in early 1995. "This is my country. These are my people. This is my extended family." A nation that knew him chiefly as a backbencher bent on confrontation was surprised when Speaker Gingrich devoted much of his swearing-in speech to the tragedies of inner-city children. But he has been working on the problem for years.

He is fond of putting himself in the place of the inner-city seven-year-old, a child used to violence, in a home without books, and, in too many cases, an unhappy young mother. The child watches television programs that portray businessmen as evil, politicians on the take, and policemen taking bribes. (He calls television "the wasteland of cynicism.") "If you're a little kid today who reads too much or speaks English that's too good, you get beaten up," he says.

The inner-city child lives in a neighborhood where so few people are employed that the work ethic is an abstraction that can't be grasped. If a welfare recipient tries to work, she is told it's illegal. Personal savings also put welfare benefits at risk. And beyond all that is a leadership cadre complaining about the debt owed it by society. All this flies in the face of Newt's vision of American civilization. Gingrich is fond of noting, for instance, that New Hampshire's state motto is "Live Free or Die," not "Live Free or Whine."

Gingrich is so frustrated by what he sees that he muses about kindergartens as boot camps.

"What's the most successful training program for the underclass?" he mused in an interview. "It's the Marine Corps boot camp. What does a Marine Corps boot camp tell you about first grade for kids in a poor neighborhood? If you really wanted to reshape the society, you'd find a way to get really first-class veterans moving into public housing and you'd say, here, you be the leader."

For all the depressing weight of his reflections on the inner city, Gingrich is at heart an optimist. Hard work and learning are the keys to the situation. Incentives are critical.

"Reward what you want to encourage," he says. "Punish or make more expensive what you want to discourage. How's that for turning the welfare and tax codes on their heads?"

Newt often quotes a study showing that more than half of first-generation millionaires interviewed had begun their first job by the time they were 10. Effectiveness comes from a set of learned habits. Middle-class parents routinely create incentives. They reward children with allowances, gifts, and trips if the child achieves certain goals. The inner-city child is surrounded by negative incentives. The drug dealer drives a Mercedes while the teacher rides the bus.

T W O - W AY S T R E E T ■ A key to Gingrich's solutions for the inner cities is that those stuck in the culture of poverty must be ready to accept responsibility, both as citizens and as managers of their own lives. He grows angry when liberal Democrats complain that a growing economy has created only "hamburger-flipping jobs." In his view, any job beats welfare.

"My answer is, " he said in 1994, "if it's the first job you've got and it gets you to work on time and you stay and earn a paycheck, it is a terrific first job. There are no bad first jobs. And every time somebody scorns any job, they're undermining the work ethic of the whole country. Any job is a good job if the alternative is no job....It's from no job to a better job. It's not like Jethro on 'The Beverly Hillbillies.' It's not from no job to brain surgeon. And if you listen to some people on the welfare state, their attitude is, 'Boy, if we don't make you a brain surgeon, you shouldn't work.' Okay?"

For years, liberals have responded to that sort of self-help as if it were myth. How can you ask someone to lift themselves up by their bootstraps, they ask, if they have no boots? In 1994 Gingrich found a response in the work of Dr. Marvin Olasky, author of the 1992 book *The Tragedy of Modern Compassion*. A professor at the University of Texas at Austin, Olasky draws on studies of 19th-century efforts to help the poor. He lays out a plan to remake both public and private charitable efforts. In 1995, Gingrich restructured his lectures to build on the ideas of *The Tragedy of Modern Compassion*, whose author advocates tying all charitable assistance to a work-reward system run largely by volunteers and involving close personal contact.

What Gingrich advocates can look likes traditional rugged individualism married to public and private efforts to see that it flourishes. But make no mistake: His rugged individualism isn't social Darwinism. He believes the lone-cowboy icon of American history is nonsense.

"There were very few loners," he says. "There was tremendous individualism, but it was individualism within groups. It was individualism within the wagon train, individualism within the community, individualism within the group of people herding the cows."

Gingrich emphasizes that if such a system were in place, those facing real adversity—the handicapped, the aged—could be targeted for effective assistance in the form of compensatory education and rehabilitation. A key word is temporary. Gingrich spotlights those few governmental units around the nation that have dropped such titles as welfare and social services. One, in Rochester, New York, has renamed the welfare office the Department of Temporary Assistance. The name makes its point.

HAVING MY BABY ▪ Any discussion of poverty in this country must include the problem of teen pregnancy. When Gingrich addresses the issue, he draws upon the findings of Leon Dash as described in his book, *When Children Want Children: The Urban Crisis of Teenage Childbearing*. Dash, an African-American reporter, lived for 18 months in a low-income area of Washington. He began his work assuming that the high incidence of teenage pregnancy among inner-city blacks was due to ignorance of birth control methods and manipulation of girls by boys.

Dash found that he was wrong on all counts. Boys and girls were receiving sex education and understanding it. Girls often wanted to have a child. "A baby," Dash wrote, "is a tangible achievement in an otherwise dreary and empty future."

And for boys, the birth of a baby is a rite of passage. Dash found that the poorest students were at highest risk of becoming pregnant or becoming a father. "If the crisis of black teenage parents was simply a matter of ignorance," Dash wrote, "then it might be relatively easy to solve, but poor academic preparation that begins in elementary school, the poverty that surrounds them and social isolation from mainstream American life motivate many of these boys and girls to have children."

Gingrich quotes a study that looked at two groups of people and three characteristics: those who finished high school, got married, and reached 20 years of age before having a child, and those who didn't.

Of the children of those in the first group, only eight percent were living in poverty in 1992. Among the second group, the dropouts and teenaged mothers, the poverty rate was 79 percent. Few would argue with the data, but making the message stick with young people is difficult. Gingrich admits it.

"It may be self-defining," he says. "People who have that discipline will succeed. People who don't have that discipline may not have discipline at succeeding either. But those two numbers I thought were devastating ."

WHATEVER WORKS ▪ Like Jack Kemp, Gingrich favors tenant ownership of public housing. But he goes further. He would end public housing. He would create enterprise zones with tax breaks for those who create jobs. He would crack down on deadbeat dads. He would make it tough on criminals by raising the odds they will get caught committing a crime. As for prisons, any decommissioned military base would be sufficient to pick up the slack.

"This [the inner city] is a real subculture. You don't woo people out of a subculture unless you use very powerful inducements and very powerful punishments. People don't leave the subculture they know voluntarily, whether it's a Welsh coal mining village, the ghetto, or rural life in West Virginia. If you're really serious about changing the culture of poverty, you have to have a very systematic approach."

Gingrich is fascinated by programs that work. He embraces the back-to-basics approach of Marva Collins' private Westside Preparatory School in Chicago and the for-profit job placement efforts for welfare recipients of America Works in New York City. He spotlights former President Jimmy Carter's Atlanta Project, a public-private effort to empower people and neighborhoods to take control of their lives. (Gingrich continued to plug Carter's project even after the former president said he prayed for Gingrich's defeat in November, 1994. Carter later said he was just using a figure of speech.)

Those ideas have been the subject of public attention, from "60 Minutes" to television movies of the week. Gingrich would try them all and more. "At the Normandy invasion," he said in an interview for this book, "we needed mass. We landed 100,000 men at one point. We couldn't land 10,000 men at 10 points and be successful. They'd have been cut to pieces. Until you get to critical mass and when people begin to see alternatives for their lives, it won't work."

Gingrich is a fanatic about the importance of reading. His Earning By Learning program, created with his friend, Dr. Mel Steely, now operates in 17 states, run by volunteers and backed by a national foundation paying children $2 for each book they read. The program places the kids with stable adult volunteers who question them to confirm that they've read the books. The Speaker uses the program in his lectures to suggest one way to break the culture of poverty. It provides poor children the kinds of incentives that middle-class children often receive from parents.

In March of 1995, Earning by Learning went a step further. The Moten School in the District of Columbia has picked up the program, tying it into a computer program that can test youngsters on 7,000 different books. It is the perfect Gingrich venture. The school is so decrepit that when it rains, library books are damaged. Yet the eager youngster responding to incentives can range far beyond the school's library offerings. Gingrich knows that reading alone won't solve the problems of inner cities. But that he suggests it so often is an indicator of how great the task and how few the programs and policies that can change individual behavior.

R I G H T S   A N D   R E S P O N S I B I L I T I E S   ▪ There are few enough jobs in the inner city. To create those jobs, Gingrich says that the American notion of entrepreneurial free enterprise must be grafted back into the cities. He uses the word entrepreneur in its original and broadest sense: to undertake. To try something. He doesn't urge everyone to go out and start a business, but to begin each day with a plan, an undertaking. It is the alternative to helplessness and victimization.

The Speaker pinpoints five enemies of entrepreneurship: bureaucracy, credentialing, taxation, litigation, and regulation. Any efforts to save the cities must start there, just as does the Contract With America. The bureaucracies stop welfare recipients from earning extra money. They stop enterprise by demanding credentials, and they create red tape that daunts most people. Individuals must be free to manage themselves, as Peter Drucker described it in a favorite Gingrich work, *The Effective Executive*.

It is here that Gingrich's arguments are the weakest, for many inner-city children aren't near the kinds of businesses, such as fast-food places, that can provide even an entry to the work force. There is hope but no proof that reining in bureaucrats, reforming the tax code, and cutting through red tape will be enough to spur development. It is also problematic for Gingrich that while he talks about preparing for the Third Wave information society, many in our inner cities missed participation in the Second Wave—the industrial, manufacturing society.

Gingrich knows that the going won't be easy. The menu of projects to defeat the cycle of poverty has a mixed record. Earning By Learning, for example, is limited to the young. Grander schemes such as Carter's Atlanta Project have been troubled by internal division and almost no measurable output. The America Works firm that finds jobs for welfare recipients in New York, admittedly hampered by state restrictions, still hasn't proven itself to be a model for privatization of the system nationally. Few are going to rely on a few projects to replace the culture of poverty and violence.

Gingrich himself seemed to have recognized that problem in

1994. It was Olasky who not only supplied a historical base for Gingrich's suspicions about why the welfare state wasn't working, but also offered some compelling solutions. Olasky's *The Tragedy of American Compassion* attempts to plug the holes between government failures and the shortage of private charitable efforts (many of them rendered meaningless by government). Olasky, who also is editor of *World*, a Christian news magazine, demands that efforts to combat poverty have a spiritual base. Bonding and affiliation are the terms he uses to describe the close-knit efforts that are needed. He offers up a mixture of government and private approaches using a sort of "tough love" mentality. Sometimes, charity must be denied. Cash to an alcoholic goes to drink in too many cases. The poor and the troubled must be reunited with families and friends, not the anonymous hand of government. Above all, demands must be made of the recipient.

"Many of the homeless have had jobs," writes Olasky, "but they just do not want to stick to them. When we hand out food and clothing indiscriminately, aren't we subsidizing disaffiliation? Other questions: Do government and private programs increase the likelihood that a pregnant, unmarried teenager will be reunited with those on whom she actually is dependent, whether she wishes to admit it or not—parents, the child's father—or do they offer a mirage of independence? Do programs encourage single parenting? Do fathers now effectively have the choice of providing or not providing?"

Olasky's historical overview emboldened Gingrich in devising his most recent lecture series. Working in 1994 with Jane Fortson, a former chairman of the Atlanta Housing Authority board and now a fellow at the Progress & Freedom Foundation, Gingrich came up with a program that supplied a framework for individual effort and faith. The plan can be seen as a road map to where Gingrich may try to lead Congress after it finishes its work on the Contract With America.

To some, the program might appear a bureaucratic list. To those who have looked at Gingrich's long study of the inner city, each item has meaning. He calls for individual and community responsibility and involvement; productivity and safety; putting children first; creating diverse communities; compassion and volunteerism; and an effective and appropriate role for government.

As for government? The new House Speaker summed it up:

"I mean, if government, frankly, could just provide public safety, and have a tax code that encouraged job creation and minimized the bureaucratic destruction of jobs, and be in a position to ensure that public learning took place whether it was in a public bureaucracy or not, government would have done all it needs to do in the inner city."

THE MAN

"[I was given] an article when I was young. It was about Lincoln's five defeats. I carried it in my wallet for years. Churchill was the same way, a man who lost a lot. It came to me that the number-one characteristic in politics is to persist until you get lucky."

CHAPTER 5

"TO PERSIST UNTIL YOU GET LUCKY"

"Personal strength can be defined as seven key aspects: integrity, courage, hard work, perseverance, discipline, responsibility, and respect for others. I'm going to walk you through each of them for just a minute, because I want you to have this sense of what's involved.

First of all, integrity. None of us are saints—I didn't put in sainthood here. All of us fudge; I understand that. That's to be human. But you have to set a core standard of integrity in a free society, starting with business transactions. If I give you a check, it has—if most checks in our society were counterfeit and most credit cards were stolen, the whole system would collapse and we'd go back to gold coins. I mean, to have a free society, you have to have a very high level of integrity.

Second is courage. And courage isn't always battlefield courage. It's just as difficult to have bureaucratic courage as to have battlefield courage. It's just as difficult to stand up for what you believe in your family or in your neighborhood or in your church or synagogue as it is sometimes to be a soldier or sailor or airman, and yet if you don't have the courage to believe something, if you don't have the courage, for example, to go out and look for a job—I mean, you look for jobs, you get turned down. You look for more jobs. It takes courage.

You've got to find it within you to go out and keep being active and keep being busy, and I think it takes courage for you to go meet new people. Those of you who have moved to a new area know what I'm talking about. You know, you find out there's a local clique.

I'll give you an example. It's sort of silly, but when I was in about the seventh or eighth grade, I lacked the courage to ask girls to dance. I don't know if any of you ever had this experience when you were very young, but my attitude was two bad things could happen if you walked across the room and you asked a girl to dance. One is she could turn you down. You then feel totally inferior, rejected, and like a jerk. The other is she could say 'yes.' You'd then be out dancing on the floor, people would notice you.

So there were two definite bad things, and it was better to stay with the guys over on this side and not talk. And again, I'm talking about things that are very human. But isn't it also true that even something as simple as asking somebody to dance takes a level of courage that we tend to take for granted.

The third characteristic is hard work. I didn't just put down 'work.' I said 'hard work.' Maybe I should have put down 'very hard work.' We undervalue what it takes to survive and prosper in a free society. We don't tell the poor the truth, which is, to be middle class is to work hard. To be middle class is to do a lot of things you don't want to do.

And yet the values, the rewards, the ability to live a decent life, to plan your career, to send your kids to school, to go on a nice vacation, to have a decent home, those rewards are paid for by hard work, and there is no shortcut. And we don't teach it enough. We particularly don't teach it enough to poor people.

Hard work then leads to perseverance. Perseverance is the hard work you do after you get tired of doing the hard work you already did. Perseverance is what you do when the seventh girl turned you down for dancing and you go to the eighth girl, or boy in the modern era. Perseverance is what happens when, in my case, I ran for Congress twice and lost. I ran a third time to win. That was five years of my life.

Perseverance is what it takes to get a Ph.D. or it's what it takes to finally have saved up enough money to buy that house or to buy your first car. Without perseverance, hard work disappears. In order to have perseverance, you have to have discipline.

Again, I'm not talking about being a Marine Corps drill sergeant. I'm not talking about a professional football player doing calisthenics. But if you don't have some level of discipline that says: Yes, I'm going to get up. Yes, I'm going to get ready. Yes, I'm going to put on some clothing and go to work. Yes, I'm going to go to class. Without the discipline to make the perseverance possible to do the hard work, it doesn't happen.

In addition, you have to have a sense of responsibility. It's a hard thing to learn. I believe we should have more responsibility for younger people. I think we made a huge mistake by creating adolescence as a zone where you're too old to be a child and too young to be an adult so you have this free-floating zone where the only thing that matters is peer pressure and peer response. I think it's crazy.

Let me go out on a limb and just tell you flatly: I think it has failed. It was a 19th-century bourgeois idea to keep the kids out of the sweatshops, and it has absolutely got teenagers worrying too much about other teenagers and not worrying enough about being adults, and we'd be much better to start finding ways to put adulthood lower and to get people brought in at puberty to many more adult responsibilities, starting with money.

In addition, I think—and we talked about this a lot, and I decided I just had to add it: You have to have respect for others. Whether it's the golden rule, 'Do unto others as you'd have them do unto you,' or just a core sense of: If I'm going to have personal strength and have you respect me, I want you to have personal strength and I'll respect you, and that mutual respect is at the core of a healthy, free society.

Now, I think all of this then comes down to be the key

question for all public policy: Will this proposal help people become more responsible, more productive, and more safe so they can be prosperous and free so they can pursue happiness?"

(Newt Gingrich, from the Renewing American Civilization lectures, Reinhardt College, Waleska, Georgia, 1994)

When Kathleen Gingrich still was speaking up, before her notorious interview with Connie Chung of CBS News, she described her brief marriage to a *New York Times* reporter in words that could have been lifted straight from a Tammy Wynette song. "We were married on a Saturday and I left him on a Tuesday," she said. "I got Newtie in those three days."

The baby born June 17, 1943, was named Newton Leroy McPherson. His mother, Kathleen Daugherty McPherson, was just 17. His father, Newton C. McPherson, Jr., was away in the Navy, soon to be sued for divorce by Kathleen. The story reads like a movie script from the World War II era.

Newton and Kit, as she was known, had been married when she was just 16. It was the same year her father was killed in a car accident. Newton was 19 and a mechanic. The newlyweds' quarters were modest, to say the least—they lived in an apartment above a filling station near Harrisburg, Pennsylvania. Kit Gingrich likes the story of how she left Newton three days after her wedding, but in fact, it was several months. Newton came home after a night of carousing. He and Kit quarreled, Newton struck her, and Kit fled to her mother's house. Hummelstown, near the Pennsylvania Dutch country and 18 miles from the state capital, would be Newt's boyhood home.

FUSSED OVER BY STRONG WOMEN ■
After Gingrich was named Speaker, it became common for reporters to draw sardonic contrasts between his early life and the Ozzie and Harriet–like, 1950s lifestyle supposedly championed by conservatives. But the better comparison is

with those wartime Hollywood movies in which the young veteran comes home from the front without a job and unsure if the girl he left behind still remembers him.

The war years changed America and changed family relationships. Men from Arizona met women from Brooklyn and settled in Kansas City. Engagements were broken off, hasty marriages ended, and children often came as surprise packages from short liaisons arranged by a kid with a train ticket to basic training in his back pocket.

After her divorce, Kathleen Gingrich's prospects weren't the best, but little Newt fell into a good situation. When his mother went to work as a salesclerk and later in a war factory, he was left in the care of his grandmother, Ethel Yeater. The former teacher taught him to read, a habit he never abandoned and one that put him steps ahead of future schoolmates. Newt says he had read 500 books by the age of 10; few who know him would challenge the claim.

His father's sister, Loma, and her husband, Cal Troutman, also looked after him. They had no children and lavished presents and attention on little Newt. And Cal, a longtime Republican precinct worker, introduced him to politics, teaching him "to smile at Eisenhower on the television and turn [Adlai] Stevenson off." Many children raised primarily around adults pick up the tag of "precocious." Gingrich fit the model.

"My Aunt Loma, Aunt Louise, and my Grandma Daugherty had a lot to do with training me," he said in 1995. "I am a product in many ways of very strong women. My Grandma Daugherty had been a teacher, and because of the modern certification techniques, she only had two years of college. When they said you had to have four years...she quit teaching. I showed up and I was her only class, so I got 30 students' worth of attention and she beat into me how to read by the time I was four."

When Newt was three years old, Kit married a young Army veteran, Bob Gingrich, who had been mustered out as a corporal in 1946. Kit's mother moved in with the young family, continuing her strong influence. Bob and Kit had three other children: Susan Shurskis, four years younger than Newt; Roberta Brown, five years younger; and the baby, Candace Gingrich, 23 years Newt's junior.

Different Family Values ■ When Candace, a United Parcel Service employee, made the rounds of Capitol Hill in early 1995 as a lesbian lobbying on behalf of the homosexual rights organization, the Human Rights Campaign Fund, her meeting with Newt became a major news story. Brother and sister hugged and kissed, and Candace praised Newt for working hard to achieve a goal. With a nod to the bank of cameras and microphones, he said, "It's Washington at its most bizarre."

The Speaker never has made much of an issue of homosexuality except to oppose its promotion in schools. In an interview with a homosexual newspaper in 1994, Gingrich said, "I think our position should be toleration. It should not be promotion and it should not be condemnation."

His half-sister disagreed, telling a *Newsweek* reporter, "A leaky faucet, a barking dog—those are things you tolerate. While Newt is promoting tolerance, his colleagues are preparing anti-gay legislation."

Gingrich was unpersuaded, saying, "I am not prepared to establish a federal law that allows you to sue your employer if you end up not having a job because of a disagreement that involves your personal behavior."

Given the more than 20-year age difference between Newt and Candace, their public disagreement is less like that of close siblings and more like that between a high-profile father and a daughter experimenting with the world. "I'm not sitting here as someone who is unfamiliar with the late 20th century," he said in 1994. "I know life can be complicated."

His relationships with his other half-sisters are the sort experienced by so many mobile Americans—warm and caring, but carried on mostly with phone calls, letters, and presents on holidays. His affection for their children showed through in the opening minutes of his swearing-in speech as Speaker when he singled them out for attention on the floor of the House.

His affection for his mother, of course, was revealed to most of America when Kathleen was interviewed by Chung and volunteered—in what she believed to be an off-the-record moment—that her son had called Hillary Rodham Clinton "a bitch." Gingrich's anger at the manipulation of a 68-year-old woman was palpable and, to most Americans, justifiable. When reporters pressed him on the truth of her remarks, he bristled at the notion that they might be calling Kit a liar.

THE STRONG, SILENT TYPE ▪ Newt's relationship with his adoptive father is not so easily categorized. Bob Gingrich is as tight-lipped as Newt is talkative. He even pronounces his name differently (*Ging-rick*). The elder Gingrich has his own firm principles. He refused to attend his son's first wedding, for instance, because he thought Newt was too young to be entering into marriage.

After he and Kit were wed, Bob worked his way through Gettysburg College as a bellhop. He was enrolled in the Reserve Officer Training Corps there and was commissioned a second lieutenant in 1951. In just a few months he shipped out for Korea and the war and a career in the infantry. He would retire eventually as a lieutenant colonel. A heavy dose of amateur psychoanalysis from the press has gone into explaining Newt Gingrich's relationships with his fathers and father figures. Does he bridle at authority or respect it? Are father figures, such as the former House Republican leader, Robert Michel, to be studied or toppled? Gingrich doesn't like the idea of the latter.

"In the first place," he told me in an interview for this book, "you can make the argument that I've been very adroit all my life in getting Dutch uncles or stepfathers or whatever you want to call them, most of which was very conscious. I'm very good at serving authority when I'm in a role that's legitimately subordinate. I offer my best advice and I help. When I cross a line into a zone where I'm responsible, I answer only to God."

Newt's biological father, Newton McPherson, left the Navy, remarried, and had two other children. Newt kept in touch with him through the years and went to him when he died of lung cancer. Newt has described him proudly as a "classic kind of hard-working industrial worker" who didn't back down from a brawl in a bar.

Career military men are among the most authoritarian figures remaining in American culture. Our novels and films reinforce the image. Newt Gingrich has been quoted on one such novel, *The Great Santini*, by Pat Conroy: "I read a part of the book and couldn't finish it; it was too frightening." In fact, he found the author frightening. "I read a fair amount about the stepfather the author was developing," he told me, "and it was clear the author hated him. I was incapable of reading an entire book by an author who despises the values I believe in."

Newt was always a fan of John Wayne films. In several, "the Duke" played a tough-talking, hard-drinking military man who had been an absent father. As Newt describes it, Bob Gingrich wasn't abusive, but he laid down the rules for the household just as he was trained to do on the post. Part of the Gingrich lore is a story about when 10-year-old Newt went to his local movie house, the Royal Theater, and saw Wayne in "The Sands of Iwo Jima" four times in one day at a time his dad was off fighting in Korea. Comparisons were inescapable: "The Duke" and Bob Gingrich, both aloof and heroic. "That movie," says Newt, "most defined my personality. I grew up trying to be John Wayne at age 50. And it took me a long time to figure out that Wayne had been a kid and had grown up just the way I did. He wasn't always the hero."

Newt fought for his dad's attention one day and tested his patience the next. The son at times resented the strange male in the house, but most of the time he admired him for his military bearing and heroism. "You've got to understand what it was like," he says, "living with men who were prepared to stand and die every day and for whom the memories of World War II were fresh."

TALKING TO THE ANIMALS ▪ The Army would take the Gingriches from their familiar Pennsylvania turf in the years ahead, but not before one of Newt's deepest passions took hold. At age 10, he took a bus to Harrisburg and met with city and state officials with a plan to create a zoo. "Boy Explains Zoo Needs to State, City Leaders" read the headline of the local newspaper. The little boy with wide-ranging interests had proposed finding 300 or more supporters to finance the zoo. Government was to provide the land, "with a moat." The news clip was sent to Bob Gingrich in Korea. His response was blunt. "Keep that boy out of the newspapers," he wrote.

He couldn't keep him away from newspaper editors, however. Gingrich counts among his mentors Paul Walker, then editor of the *Harrisburg Home Star*, to whom he had gone with his zoo plans. The boy was interested in Abraham Lincoln, prompted perhaps by the Gettysburg battlefield just a few miles away.

"Walker gave me an article when I was young," Gingrich said in an interview in 1994. "It was about Lincoln's five defeats. I carried it in my wallet for years. Churchill was the same way, a man who lost a lot. It came to me that the number-one characteristic in politics is to persist until you get lucky."

When Newt was 11 years old, his dad was transferred to Fort Riley, near Junction City, Kansas. The family moved so much when Newt was growing up that the boy could rarely make lasting friends. He constantly had to summon up his courage to arrive at a new place, walk into a circle of children, introduce himself, and then establish himself.

"There is probably a part of me that's been lonely...for large parts of my life," he said in 1989. "You'd move every 18 months or so and so would your best friend, so you'd have that churning. But I do have a network of personal friends that is very deep and very real."

Those friends came later. First there were those moves. It's little wonder he read so much. Bob Gingrich bought him the *Encyclopedia Americana* and he buried himself in it. Animals and paleontology were key interests. At age 11, his seriousness was evident: When he flew home alone from Fort Riley to

Harrisburg, his plane stopped in Chicago; during the layover, the little boy hailed a taxi to visit the Lincoln Park Zoo.

His fascination with animals—from every era—continues today. Speaker Gingrich sports Tyrannosaurus Rex neckties and decorates his office with replicas of prehistoric animals on loan from the Smithsonian Institution. One of his great passions is Zoo Atlanta, to which he donated almost $40,000 over a decade. It is a considerable sum for a man whose net worth is listed on official disclosure forms at less than $110,000.

"Newt is an incredible supporter," says Dr. Terry Maple, director of Zoo Atlanta. "He has a deep and abiding concern for wildlife. He's always told me that when he finished his political career he's going to go off and become a zookeeper. I can foresee him becoming a major contributor to preserving species."

In 1993, Gingrich donated $15,000 to Zoo Atlanta for the purchase of two extremely rare large lizards called Komodo dragons. He flew them in from Washington in a private plane. At the airport that evening, Gingrich beamed with delight. My daughter Chase, then three years old, still calls him "the dragon man."

THE BONES LEFT BEHIND ▪ As a teenager, Newt's conversion from the concerns of the animal kingdom to those of the human species was a gradual one. From Kansas, the family moved in 1956 to Orleans, France, south of Paris. The postwar years, the Cold War, the armies on alert, all convinced the youngster that the world was dangerous. He still uses words like dark, brutal, and barbaric to describe civilization's potential for chaos.

The Gingrich family visited the World War I battlefield of Verdun, still scarred by shells from the war's bloodiest battle. The teenager viewed the glassed-in basement of an ossuary, a massive structure in which rested the remains of more than 100,000 unidentified soldiers that had been left rotting in the fields during nine months of battle. At that moment, his young dreams of being a zookeeper were put aside.

"I can still feel the sense of horror and reality which overcame me then," he wrote in *Window of Opportunity*. "I have never been back, yet Verdun is as real to me as if I had visited it last weekend. It is the driving force which pushed me into history and politics and molded my life."

Convinced that what happened once could happen again, the boy decided politics were to be his life. Politicians, after all, told generals what to do.

"People like me are what stand between us and Auschwitz," he has said. Critics accuse him of an excess of ego for statements like that, but it is Gingrich's shorthand. At Verdun the face of evil stared at him. But it didn't turn him to pacifism. Instead, he remembered Churchill's dictum: "War is horrible; slavery is worse."

Kids who foresee themselves saving the world don't have it easy at school. Gingrich reflects on those times with humor.

"I think I was very lonely and very driven," he recalls. "If you decide in your freshman year in high school that your job is to spend your lifetime trying to change the future of your people, you're probably fairly weird. I think I was pretty weird as a kid."

And so it was when the family moved to Stuttgart, Germany, when Newt was 15. Bob Gingrich worked in military intelligence, analyzing Soviet and East German units. Alerts were frequent in the shadow of the Iron Curtain. In high school in Germany, at an age when students today have trouble with short essays, Newt wrote a 180-page paper on the global balance of power.

B E L O W   T H E   M A S O N - D I X O N   L I N E ▪ From Stuttgart, the Gingrich family moved in 1960 to Fort Benning, Georgia, outside Columbus on Georgia's western border with Alabama. The family would go home to Pennsylvania eventually, but Newt would stay, build a political network, marry, and make the state his home. For a Northerner committed to integration, it was an odd place to put down roots.

At Baker High School (ironically, its full name was Newton

D. Baker High School), Gingrich fit that modern play on words, radical geek. Newt's Democratic opponent in 1994, Ben Jones, is prone to calling the Speaker a "wuss." Jones, a former congressman and television actor, is a basketball fanatic. Of Gingrich he says, "He won't rebound," suggesting that Gingrich doesn't do hard work. "He's the guy who won the science project," says Jones with a sneer. He did play football, however, until headaches prompted a doctor to make him leave the squad. Gingrich was more tutor than tackle. Still, he was a National Merit semifinalist who was accepted by his peers. He was voted most intellectual in his class, performed in the Thespian Society, and belonged to the debate club. A friend from the class behind his, Jackie Tillman, remembers him as being the smartest around, but popular and fun.

"You could have said he was a nerd or a geek," she recalls, "but his best friend was the student body president and he hung out with the good citizens, the popular, smart kids."

She remembers him reading voraciously, marking quotes and thoughts with a pencil. Tillman helped him copy those passages into notebooks. "He had shoeboxes filled with reference notes," she says. "He must have had 50 boxes of them, and he used them in class and in politics."

Gingrich's high school days were notable for three things: politics, the closest friendship of his life, and a very well kept secret.

His political activism began in March, 1960, his junior year at Baker High, when he volunteered in the presidential campaign of Richard Nixon. Gingrich and his classmate and closest friend, Jim Tilton, dreamed of creating a Republican majority. Jackie Tillman remembers that Newt's goal was to be the first Republican governor in Georgia since Reconstruction and then to use that prominence to vault him into presidential politics. In Georgia, that was tough sledding. Republican elected officials were as rare as snowplows.

The legacy of Reconstruction still dominated the Deep South in 1960. Georgia's governor, Ernest Vandiver, its senators, Herman Talmadge and Richard B. Russell, and every one of its congressional representatives were Democrats. It had been thus since the federal government imposed Reconstruction after the Civil War. In 1960, even a Roman Catholic, John F. Kennedy, could carry Georgia for the Democratic Party. Nixon's chief support came from the black wards, still loyal to the party of Lincoln and federal patronage. It would be four years before a Republican would be acceptable to whites along the racial fault line that was Southern politics.

The situation was the perfect challenge for an outlander who was a student of Gettysburg, the beginning of the end for the South in the war. He volunteered for the Nixon campaign and had his first taste of political defeat. Jackie Tillman was Catholic, Democratic, and a Kennedy supporter.

"I remember being shocked that he was a Republican," says Tillman. "I'm not sure I'd ever met one before. Newt was shaken after Nixon's loss. He took it hard. He had studied Nixon's career, how he was from a family of modest means. It was one of the reasons Newt played football, because Nixon did and he thought it was the right thing to do for political reasons. After Nixon lost, I started to kid him, but he was so serious. 'Jackie, if only 100,000 more people had voted or changed their vote, Nixon would be president.' I took one look at Newt's face and decided not to tease on this one."

Gingrich ran the winning campaign for student body president of his closest friend, Jim Tilton. They dreamed and schemed together. Tilton's death from cancer in 1993 was a moment more painful for Gingrich than any of his political setbacks, one that moved him to rare public tears.

TEACHER'S PET ■ Throughout that senior year, Newt was keeping a major secret, going off alone to make hushed phone calls that were the subject of speculation among his friends. He was dating Jackie Battley, his 24-year-old geometry teacher. Gingrich had told his friend Tilton on the first day he saw her in class that he was going to marry her. The boy reared a Lutheran and preached to by Methodist military chaplains became a Southern Baptist to please her. To avoid the glare of their hometown, Newt and

Jackie went on dates to cities in Alabama.

"Everybody knew he had a girl," Jackie Tillman said, "but it was a secret. He talked about her, but we couldn't learn who it was. I finally figured it out when I went to Miss Battley after class to ask her a question and I saw a letter on her desk about a teaching job in Atlanta, where Newt was going to go to college. It figured. She was smart and very peppy and she was different. She drank hot tea, which wasn't common around there."

Jackie Tillman's guess was right. Gingrich took some courses after high school at Columbus College and then went to suburban Atlanta to attend Emory University, one of the South's finest schools. Jackie followed him there, and the couple was married in a bittersweet ceremony after his freshman year. Bob Gingrich refused to attend, believing the boy too young and the seven-year age difference too great. Kit Gingrich, who carried the memory of her short first marriage, agreed with her husband. The Gingrich sisters stayed home as well.

"If you live your life hostage to everybody else's decision," he told the *Washington Post* years later, "you either have to live a very narrow life or you have to spend a lot of time in pain. I hoped my mother would come....I never held it against her. I never held it against him."

The boy Gingrich quickly became a man, with the responsibilities of fatherhood. Some high-school friends still believe that Newt pursued Jackie because he wanted an anchor and because, in his grand political ambition, he needed a wife and family. Others settle on a simpler belief: He was intellectually mature beyond his years and needed a woman of accomplishment from whom he could learn. And, of course, it could have been even simpler, for who knows what sparks the hearts —or hormones—of teenaged boys?

He was 19 when they married. Nine months later their first daughter, Linda Kathleen, now Kathy Lubbers, was born. Jacqueline Sue, now Jackie Zyla, was born three and a half years later.

POLITICS THAT COUNTED ■ Gingrich began at Emory as a political science major, but added history so that he could complete a double major. "History allowed me to to go in search of sheer data and make my own analysis," he said.

His classroom work suffered, in part because he was married and a father and holding down part-time jobs, but mainly because he was a nearly full-time political organizer.

Gingrich founded the Emory chapter of the Young Republicans and worked to put Edward Smith on the ballot as the Republican candidate for governor in 1962, but Smith was killed in a car accident. (In that year, as in 1958, the governor's race was decided in the Democratic primary.) After Smith died, the Georgia GOP was $50,000 in debt and unable to hire staff.

The ambitious college kid got himself appointed the party's part-time executive director. The position allowed him to travel the state, making contacts and listening to voters. In 1963, he helped develop the concept of a traveling platform committee, an early version of the Contract With America. The idea was to have a document through which candidates, particularly the inexperienced ones, could articulate a message.

His travels led him in 1964 to a job as campaign manager for a Republican congressional candidate. Jack Prince was running against the popular Democrat, Phil Landrum, in the mountain and lake area north of Atlanta. It was a mismatch. The college student whose roots were in Pennsylvania faced off against Landrum's campaign manager, Ed Jenkins, a son of the Georgia mountains who would go on to his own long congressional career.

The political tempest of the moment was chickens, their export tied up with nuclear politics among France, the U.S., and the Soviet Union. With poultry production the district's largest industry, Gingrich urged Prince to put chickens ahead of international issues in his campaign. Before the Gainesville Jaycees, Prince did just that, but Landrum trumped him.

"I'm not going to swap chickens today," he said, "for nuclear bombs tomorrow." Gingrich and his candidate were soundly defeated. Prince's was the only congressional district in Georgia that the Republican presidential candidate, Barry Goldwater, failed to carry. Gingrich learned not to fully trust the late Tip O'Neill's adage that "all politics are local." And he learned about the well-chosen phrase.

The chastened collegian went back to Emory with a new perspective. Republicans were gaining a foothold in Georgia, but it would be a long uphill battle. The Democrats gave their foes an opening the next year. It was 1965, the year Newt Gingrich marks as the modern equivalent of 1860, when the South fired on Fort Sumter, South Carolina. President Lyndon Johnson, supported by a nation grieving the assassination of John Kennedy and the violence spawned by the civil rights movement, was passing the social welfare programs of his Great Society over the objections of the once Solid South.

"He had an accidental majority," Gingrich believes, "that allowed him to ram this program through Congress. It shattered the Democratic Party forever. And he could not defend his Vietnam War. That launched the counterculture that has been so destructive."

That year, Gingrich received his degree from Emory. He chortles now that for all his childhood precociousness, he wasn't a diligent student. His grade-point average was a modest 2.8.

"I'd flunked an English lit course on the short story," he said in 1995, "and I failed a political science course because I was late to the final. I'd been talking to a potential candidate for governor."

Despite those modest grades and a pair of F's, Gingrich scored high on the Graduate Record Examination. He believes his scores changed his life.

"I'd always assumed I was about to become a bank clerk," he recalls. But his test scores won him a National Defense Education Act fellowship to Tulane University, a respected school in New Orleans often referred to as part of a Southern ivy league.

FATHERING, NOT SOLDIERING ▪ By 1966, Vietnam draft calls were increasing, but Newt and Jackie had two young daughters. They earned him a deferment from the draft, but he of course had the option to volunteer. Newt supported the war effort, and not simply because Bob Gingrich was serving in counterguerrilla operations in Vietnam. But, he said once, it would have been irrational for him to volunteer and leave two young daughters behind.

Over the years, I've heard Newt Gingrich say many times that he wishes he had volunteered. Whatever his feelings were in the middle and late 1960s—and if he was like most young men in his age group they changed more than once—Gingrich never was at risk of being inducted. The accusations of draft-dodging by his political foes ring hollow. And comparisons with Bill Clinton, who was consumed by finding the least politically damaging way to avoid service, are an exercise in apples and oranges.

At Tulane, Gingrich stepped into the activism of the era. He also tacked into some political winds that have caused others to question the consistency of his beliefs. Tulane was then an established training ground for Southern gentlemen. Like most private schools of the era, it paid little attention to the community around it. Student activism was focusing on the stark contrasts between student affluence and the poverty of the black neighborhoods of New Orleans.

Gingrich took a brief turn at taking on the establishment, though not in the radical and often criminal manner that protests were conducted on many campuses at the time. He led protests over the administration's refusal to allow the school newspaper, the *Hullaballoo*, to print nude photographs.

He was an odd radical, if the term is even accurate. He wore jackets and ties to class, was married to a very conservative woman, and had little interest in popular culture. He has admitted to smoking marijuana one time, saying "It didn't have any effect on me."

Newt completed his master's degree in modern European history and spent a year in Belgium to complete his dissertation on "Belgian Education Policy in the Congo, 1945–1960." But his political activities always came first. He was Louisiana cochair of the Nelson Rockefeller campaign for the Republican presidential nomination in 1968. Some coworkers say he chose Rockefeller only because he disliked Nixon. Gingrich recalls that he made a major league blunder: He did not believe Nixon was electable. Still, Rockefeller had the more attractive position on civil rights for Gingrich, who was sending one of his daughters to a largely black day care center and trying to recruit blacks to the GOP cause.

The segregation of Columbus, Georgia, had troubled him, coming as he did from a family of the Army, an integrated meritocracy. Jackie Tillman recalls that she and Newt were angry each day when the school buses from Fort Benning stopped outside the post so that black students could catch another bus to a segregated high school.

His opposition to the Tulane administration, his growing belief that cultural elites were at odds with American values, his civil rights advocacy, his lessened support for the Vietnam War, and his support for Rockefeller have led critics to suggest opportunism. But each position had its own rationale. He grew to oppose the war, for instance, because it was being prosecuted by politicians and couldn't be won.

INTO A DEMOCRATIC STRONGHOLD ■
In 1970, the new Dr. Newton L. Gingrich, Ph.D., decided where home was: West Georgia College, 35 miles west of Atlanta in the town of Carrollton. It was a good place for a man with one eye on academia and the other on politics. Jackie Battley Gingrich's family was nearby in Columbus. Professor Gingrich had his high-school friends there. Atlanta, with its press and levers of political power, was an easy drive away down Interstate 20. He was 27 years old, with a home in several worlds and a choice of careers. He was a serious student and writer and he loved to teach and motivate, but the political passions never waned. Yet the politician in him faced a daunting political landscape.

Paul Coverdell, elected to the U.S. Senate from Georgia in 1992, remembers how bleak it was for Republicans then. "In 1970," he wrote me, "not long after I entered the state senate as one of only four GOP senators, I joined with a West Georgia college professor and a businessman from St. Simons Island to discuss how a two-party system could become a reality in Georgia." Gingrich—with two men who would go to the U.S. Senate, Coverdell and Mack Mattingly—was resuming the political organizing he had done in his days at Emory almost a decade before.

The area around Carrollton was true "yellow-dog Democrat country." But the Democratic Party's increasing domination by its liberal wing was causing some changes. In 1970, the year Gingrich moved to West Georgia College, a leading Democrat, Jimmy Bentley, was among several Georgia politicians who switched parties.

Bentley, the state comptroller and a protégé of Sen. Herman Talmadge, was perfectly positioned to beat Jimmy Carter in the general election for governor. But Bentley was defeated in the Republican primary by Hal Suit, a respected Atlanta television news anchor. Carter defeated Suit handily. Bentley recalls that at the time there really was no Republican Party; there were only pockets of voters in a few suburbs.

"I asked the state party for a list of contacts," Bentley recalls, "and I set off across the state. I'd go into a town expecting a greeting and I'd find a postmaster with a federal job and no organization."

The district around Carrollton was no different. A few years later, the state representative from nearby Bremen, Thomas B. Murphy, would be chosen Speaker of the Georgia House. He was still in that post in 1995, the longest-tenured speaker in the nation. Twenty-five years ago, even the Atlanta suburbs on the city's south and west sides were inhospitable to Republicans. Newt had picked not a political launching pad but a prickly thicket.

THE AMBITIOUS PROFESSOR ■ Gingrich began in Carrollton as the teacher more than the politician, taking over a Western Civilization course his first year. Students loved the man with dark hair, bushy sideburns well below his ears, and metal-rim glasses. West Georgia wasn't

Berkeley, but the turmoil of the 1960s had made itself felt, opening up traditional academic disciplines to less traditional courses. Gingrich, never shy, found he could spark change.

Older faculty members held their tongues as the young teacher launched an environmental studies course, continued the study of the future he'd begun at Tulane, and even dabbled in humanistic psychology, a left-coast sort of discipline not common in Georgia.

Students loved the new stuff and got up at dawn to make Gingrich's 7 A.M. class. Their professor organized a chapter of the Georgia Conservancy and led students on walks to observe the impact of pollution. His futurist course introduced them to Alvin and Heidi Toffler and *Future Shock*. Classes toured the Okefenokee Swamp, and students and teacher drank beer together. In a precursor to the Renewing American Civilization lectures of the 1990s, Gingrich teamed with two of his closest friends to teach contemporary history. Dr. Mel Steely, now his authorized biographer, and Floyd Hoskins, now retired, teamed with Gingrich to take on the world and its problems. Gingrich lectured on America, Steely taught about Europe, and Hoskins specialized in Asia. Their debates were memorable for the students, most of them from small Georgia communities.

A few faculty members saw Gingrich as self-centered and manipulative, but his students were delighted to have an outlet for the rebelliousness of the time. He would debate anything, anytime, anywhere. He was open to new ideas and eager to speculate about the future. He wasn't published in scholarly journals, however, and that gave his faculty foes long-term ammunition. His opponents also were aided by his eclectic interests. Newt could not settle down with one subject for very long.

Newt first marked himself as a bull in the faculty coffee shop in 1971 when he wrote an unsolicited paper for the school's presidential search committee on what sort of person should lead West Georgia into the future. It was a bold move for a new man on campus. A year later, he sought the chairmanship of the history department, losing out to Albert

S. Hanser, who was recruited from Vanderbilt University. Steve Hanser became Gingrich's role model, friend, and confidant, the person to whom Newt still turns for advice on campaigns or designing his college lectures. They've been debating each other for 25 years.

FROM CLASSROOM TO CAMPAIGN ▪ In 1974, Gingrich traded political theory for political reality, offering himself as Republican candidate for Georgia's Sixth Congressional District against an entrenched power. The Sixth District, of which Carrollton was a part, had been represented for 20 years by Rep. John J. (Jack) Flynt, a man typical of the conservative Democrats who dominated Southern politics. They had segregationist pasts and owed their allegiances to a dozen or more county courthouses, with their commissioners, sheriffs, clerks, and other employees. Patronage jobs were important in many rural communities, where government jobs and farming were the only career options.

Gingrich saw that the Sixth District was changing—the growing metropolitan area of Atlanta was spreading its way. He attacked Flynt as a symbol of entrenched corruption and a keeper of the status quo. To avoid the Republican tag where it was anathema, he ran as a populist, attacking special interests. He was on the ballot as a Republican, but his campaign materials never featured that fact. He insisted that his staff and volunteers describe him as a moderate. Next to Flynt, he was. On racial issues he was downright liberal by the standards of the South at that time. Gingrich made public his personal finances and refused to accept contributions larger than $1,000. He questioned Flynt's ethics for paying a part-time congressional clerk's salary to the manager of his farm for 17 years.

In the spirit of what was then a young ecology movement, Gingrich labeled Flynt one of the nation's "dirty dozen" on the environment. He also took on the district's largest employer, calling Southwire a polluter. (Southwire later became a large contributor to Gingrich's campaigns and political action committee.) His changing relationship with

Southwire, which employed thousands and owned the newspaper and a bank in Carrollton, later would leave Gingrich open to charges of acting more for political expediency than principle.

With a flock of young college volunteers and an effort to reach out to minorities and union members, Gingrich was learning how to build a machine while still carrying the label of reformer. He told the *Atlanta Journal* that year that his ambition was "to be an old-time political boss in 20 years." In just a few years, he was to be a new kind of political boss.

The election was a squeaker. Gingrich lost by only two percentage points. He was done in not by lack of effort or strategy, but by Washington. The Watergate scandal of Richard Nixon caused the largest turnover in congressional history until the Gingrich revolution of 1994. Newt was undaunted in defeat, heading back into the classroom and working even harder to keep together the coalitions he had built. For his next race against Flynt in 1976, he raised $135,000, $50,000 more than in his first campaign. The national Republican Party, staggering after Watergate, had positioned Gingrich as sort of the new face of the GOP. It kicked in $25,000 in hopes of breaking the Democratic lock on Georgia's congressional delegation. He again lost, however, this time by 50.9 percent to 49.1 percent.

But the candidate had seen the defeat coming many months before, when Jimmy Carter won Wisconsin's Democratic presidential primary in April and seemed assured of the nomination. Carter wasn't a dominating presidential candidate nationally, but he was Georgia's native son. Gingrich said it made him run even harder, to get through another defeat and on to 1978. "I literally ran the entire year just to survive."

Gingrich surely had to summon up all his personal motivation techniques to watch as joyous Georgia Democrats swarmed over Washington for the inauguration of one of their own. He also had to remain upbeat and motivate his supporters with the power of his ideas, lest he be perceived as a perennial loser.

His post-election interview with the *Atlanta Journal* was revealing.

"I think there are parts of the district that are even more traditonal than I realized, and a Republican, no matter how concerned he is, cannot win a black precinct....I don't know that I have a political career. I'm a college teacher who ran twice for Congress."

He soon rebounded. Every passing year meant more hospitable turf for a Republican in west Georgia. Jack Flynt saw it as well. Change was coming, and he was facing an indefatigable opponent whose attacks escalated each time out. Flynt could count. He remembered the narrow margin of the Watergate year. He saw that Gingrich ran two-to-one ahead of his presidential nominee, Vice President Gerald Ford, in 1976. It was time to retire.

CHARACTER QUESTIONS ▪ The 1978 campaign was to spark charges that Gingrich is a hypocrite, a leaf in the political winds. Former aides such as Lee Howell and Kip Carter, whose stints with the candidate and congressman ended badly, are quick to accuse him of changing course. Howell, a speechwriter and press aide, was a former student at West Georgia who saw in Gingrich a moderate fighting against a candidate of the Old South. Howell wanted change, but he never was comfortable with a Republican. Similar reactions came from a few colleagues at West Georgia who saw only a moderate environmentalist and were surprised to learn of Gingrich's conservative leanings. Kip Carter, a former campaign manager, has portrayed Gingrich as a man whose every move, including his divorce, was for his own political advantage.

More ideological colleagues, such as former aide Frank Gregorsky, now a stalwart conservative theorist in Washington, believe times changed more than Gingrich did. Labels are applied differently today. As the Great Society has deteriorated, Gregorsky thinks, anti-government sentiment has become more widespread. And Gingrich himself had a more optimistic view of government in 1976 than he did in 1994. T.

Rogers Wade, the administrative assistant to Senator Talmadge and now a public affairs consultant, agrees that the times, not the man, shifted.

"He hasn't changed since he walked into my office in Washington in 1975 looking for help and advice and I told him he was in the wrong office," Wade told me. "I've found him to be the most consistent political animal I've ever met."

In 1978, the Democrats in waiting jumped at Flynt's seat. Two respected legislators, Peter Banks and state Sen. Virginia Shapard, qualified. They were joined by the far better known Betty Talmadge, a successful businesswoman and feisty ex-wife of the senator. Their bitter divorce, with its revelations of campaign cash stuffed in overcoat pockets, sparked the ethics hearings that led to U.S. Senate censure of Talmadge. Against each of them, Gingrich was an outsider, a Yankee. And he certainly wasn't as well known as Mrs. Talmadge.

Shapard emerged from the Democratic primary to take on the Republican. She was far less conservative than Flynt and targeted her message to women. But a far different Newt Gingrich was ready for her. The "college teacher who ran twice for Congress" was replaced by a sophisticated politician who had to win. West Georgia College was all but behind him, and the stakes now were those of a career.

He needed a victory.

CHAPTER 6

PROFESSOR GINGRICH TAKES WASHINGTON

"It is one day at a time with continuous improvement. That's the key to success. You've got to do a little bit every day. You've got to try to improve every day. You don't get this done in a big jump forward. You get it done one step at a time.

And again, every time you run into people, they say, 'Well, that doesn't get you very far.' No, but it's the right direction. It's the right movement. There's no hamburger-flipping job. Any job beats welfare. Because it's a step, it's the beginning. It's where you get started.

Now, in that framework, you want to build on opportunity and success, not focus on problems and failure. This is going to be one of my greatest challenges this year in the Congress, is convincing our committees to have hearings on success. What are the 10 best addiction reform programs in America? What are the 10 best schools in America? What works? So people can copy what works, not just study the pathologies.

And next, and this one will obviously be—fit my personality, or at least my experience: Do not shy away from controversy. This is a choice between two value systems, two power structures, and two visions of America. Conflict is inevitable and direct. Blunt debate is desirable. That until you're prepared to engage the issue of personal strength and talk honestly about what it implies, you're not going to get anywhere, and that, by definition, is going to be controversial.

Now, let me give you some examples. I would suggest

*that in American Civilization, that Americans favor
work over idleness, saving over debt, family over
individual chaos, helping your children over abandon-
ment, responsibility over irresponsibility, learning over
ignorance, and responsible citizenship over indifference.
In every case, my point—this is not just nice words—my
point is in each case, the law and the government should
favor the former over the latter. That is, you ought to
literally go through the tax code, the welfare code, the
bureaucratic rules and regulations. You should go
through the entire structure of government and say: Are
we sending signals that favor work over idleness? That
favor saving over debt? That strengthen family over
individual chaos? That give you an incentive and a legal
structure to help children rather than abandon them?
How are we doing this?*

*Or, in fact, do we, without even realizing it, send the
opposite signal? Go to work and we'll tax you and we'll
kick you off Medicaid. Save and we'll raise your Social
Security taxes. Try to get married and the earned income
tax credit will take $4,600 away from you.*

*Try to adopt a child and it can cost up to $50,000 to
adopt a child, so they're trapped in foster care and they're
trapped—and, you know, people attacked me over the
orphanage argument. This is a society which has
artificially made it expensive to adopt children. Just the
opposite of a good, strong pro-family environment.*

*Now, the reason I said we should look at the law and
the government is because the law is a great teacher. And
I really don't think you can fully appreciate the power of
this. You know when a teacher is saying, 'You ought to
work hard,' and out in the yard there's an illiterate drug
dealer driving a Cadillac, then the law is tolerating a
lesson to be taught. And no matter how often you say it
in the classroom, it's not going to work.*

*So you've got to structure the law so that you are
learning from your government and society what you
wish to teach in the classroom. And if the classroom is*

teaching one thing and government and society is teaching another, you should assume that at best, you're going to have conflict. And, at worst, that the ultimate reality of the society will drown in the classroom. It doesn't do any good to say, 'Let's teach it to them' if the law doesn't teach it too.

And so you've got to think about the law as a teacher. In addition, frankly, leaders can be teachers. It's very, very important to recognize that leaders play a very, very important role, and the way they model, what they say, where they go is important.

Part of this process of teaching: Do you go to the Boy Scout jamboree or not? Do you go to the Girl Scout national meeting or not? Do you think the Salvation Army is important enough to visit or not? How does a leader spend their time and where do they go and who do they see and then what do they talk about? These are important factors.

I wear a Habitat for Humanity pin. I understand the other night that on 'Saturday Night Live' that the person that caricatures me also had a Habitat pin on. But I'm sending a signal. I'm saying that Habitat for Humanity is a good program and that others ought to have a pin, too. You pick the program you like, but tell me what you're doing that's important, because these are signals. They matter. They communicate. Public symbols and awards can teach."

(Newt Gingrich, from the Renewing American Civilization lectures,
Reinhardt College, Waleska, Georgia, 1994)

The '60s got to Georgia in the '70s. As the '70s waned in Carrollton, Newt's look also changed—a little late, a lot less than hip. The hair, previewing the coming gray, was shorter. The glasses gave way to contact lenses. He was moving away from the classroom to the public stage, one election at a time.

With each campaign the opportunities for scholarly research—bringing with them the comforts of academic tenure—grew dimmer. The man who boldly sought the presidency of West Georgia College as a rookie teacher had angered many colleagues. By 1978 he had little chance of earning tenure. The people closest to him argue he never really sought it, pointing to his forays into several different disciplines and into politics.

"Jackie and Newt made a decision in November, 1973, to forego tenure," recalls colleague Mel Steely. "They decided that politics came first, but so did the knowledge that it would be seven years and out at the college. He could have pursued it. After all, he had offers from Wayne State University, and there was interest from the West Georgia geography department."

Gingrich recalls that tenure was never in his sights, and that Dean Richard Dangle agreed.

"I only thought about seeking tenure one day in my entire life," he told me. "I had one conversation with Dick Dangle over a bourbon. We were standing over the kitchen sink and I said, 'Dick, what do you think?' And he said, 'Run.' Tenure was a joke. I was going to be a political figure."

The 1978 campaign, then, was not like the two before it. Gingrich never has sought to accumulate wealth, but every family needs a living. He was broke from the two campaigns and would be off the West Georgia payroll just as the election and its heavy expenses got underway. In the hope that he could produce a lucrative novel, he arranged unconventional financing for a book project. It was to become an issue many years later.

P O L I T I C A L   H A R D B A L L   ▪ Gingrich turned to the 1978 campaign with passion, blessed by campaign contributions from national Republican officials. Volunteers gave way to paid staff. Carlyle Gregory was the campaign manager and Bob Weed the consultant. The college town was replaced as headquarters by an office in a more populous suburban Atlanta county, the largest in the Sixth District.

Many of the faculty and students who had helped him in the previous campaigns stepped aside, disheartened by what they saw as a hard turn to the right.

Any confusion about his political identity, if there ever should have been any, was erased that year. Gingrich joined the anti-tax bandwagon with a certain trumpet. In Rep. Jack Kemp, Gingrich found his model for how to appeal to old-line, blue-collar Democrats as well as Republicans. In 1978, Kemp and Sen. William Roth, the Delaware Republican, were pushing for tax cuts, echoing Dr. Arthur Laffer's supply-side argument that tax cuts would increase federal revenue. A few years later, Kemp-Roth, as it was known, would be embraced by Ronald Reagan and passed by Congress. It was sound strategy against his rival, Virginia Shapard, a state legislator who could be counted on in Washington to vote with the Democratic majority.

Most Georgia Democrats are conservative by national standards. To defeat them, Republicans must "nationalize" the campaigns, tying opponents to unpopular national issues. The tactic is used today in just about every Georgia congressional and legislative race. Find the vote against tax cuts, even the responsible ones, or the vote for a tax increase, and equate it to the liberal tax-and-spend policies of national Democrats. In 1994, for example, Gingrich allies won three Democratic congressional seats, two of them from incumbents who were done in by their votes for President Clinton's first budget and tax increases.

So it was with Shapard, who by being progressive in Georgia's sometimes prehistoric legislative politics could be portrayed as a raging liberal. Never mind that nothing in her life or career suggested that she would become a Ted Kennedy clone upon landing at Washington National Airport. She was neither a good ol' girl nor a Bella Abzug–style, radical feminist. But attack Newt did. Shapard's husband was wealthy, which added the opportunity for populist attacks familiar in Georgia (though usually made by Democrats).

While Gingrich's TV spots attacked Shapard on taxes and economic issues, less high-minded tactics were employed in

other media. Gingrich says he doesn't remember the rough
stuff, but included in the Gingrich collection in the Ingram
Library at West Georgia College is a flyer showing Shapard
with then–state Sen. Julian Bond of Atlanta, a veritable devil
to white voters outside Atlanta. "If you like welfare cheaters,"
read the caption, "You'll love Virginia Shapard." Her sin was
voting with Bond against a Republican welfare bill in the state
senate.

Another commercial noted that Gingrich would take his
wife and daughters to Washington if elected, while Shapard
planned to commute. And in time-honored Georgia fashion,
Newt was identified as a deacon in the First Baptist Church of
Carrollton, while Shapard was "a communicant" of the
Church of the Good Shepherd. Anti-Catholic prejudice long
has been a part of Georgia politics. Today, a reader is left to
wonder if the ad was a play to bigotry or a statement of fact
meant to bring comfort to Baptists, by far the largest
denomination in Georgia.

Gingrich defeated Shapard handily, no mean accomplishment in the overwhelmingly Democratic district. On election
night he signaled that he wasn't planning to be just a
representative of rural Georgia by making the rounds of the
Atlanta television stations. Their live remote trucks weren't at
his headquarters, so he came to them, competing with the
better-known Atlanta representatives for air time.

He was relaxed that night and not especially excited. When
I spoke with him, he asked the questions. What was going on
in Michigan? And California? And everywhere. We dutifully
checked the news wires for him. (By election night 1994, the
pollster Frank Luntz would have available for the new
Speaker results from 435 congressional races with just the
push of a few buttons on his cellular phone.)

On his first winning election night, Newt Gingrich began
two tugs of war. One was with himself over his marriage to
Jackie. The other was whether to tend to Georgia, his adopted
state, or exercise his obvious national ambitions. The first
would end badly. The second continues, although his move to
a new, more Republican district has eased the struggle, and his

election as Speaker has made his national interests understandable to most at home.

CHALLENGING SECOND-CLASS STATUS ▪ The new congressman went off to Washington and, as did the young professor at a new college, raced for the head of the class. He had seen the tiny, dispirited minority of Republicans in Georgia public life. He knew that young men and women, even those with Republican ideals, became Democrats in order to succeed in a one-party state. What he saw in Congress was a larger group, but still a minority, accepting of their lot in life. Theirs was to go along to get along. Republicans cut deals. For their support of a bill, they would demand modest concessions for the home folks. They tempered legislation too radical for their tastes. They cut spending bills ever so slightly and inserted provisions into tax bills to help favored constituencies.

They were the political version of the team that travels with the Harlem Globetrotters and loses gracefully at every stop. Is it only an accident that for years, that foil for the Globetrotters was named the Washington Generals?

Gingrich went to see the chairman of the National Republican Congressional Campaign Committee, Rep. Guy Vander Jagt of Michigan, urging him to develop a plan for a Republican majority. It was what he had done 18 years before as a college student.

Vander Jagt skipped over 155 more senior Republican members and gave Gingrich a task force. Gingrich told the *Atlanta Journal* that he wasn't interested in serving time and obtaining credits on subcommittees. The minority role—slogging through legislation, trying to soften its rough edges—wasn't for him. He wanted to challenge Democrats and the Republican leadership. He was out to expose the corruption of one-party rule.

To that end, he took a seat on the House Administration Committee, which then was a thankless job akin to being treasurer of the PTA. But for Gingrich it was the place to learn how the system worked. Years later, that knowledge would help him when the House Bank scandal was in full cry. Also, by accepting the less glamorous assignment, he was able to win a spot on the Public Works Committee, which oversaw Hartsfield International Airport, the most important economic engine in his district and vital to metro Atlanta's growth.

A QUESTION OF VALUES ▪ When Newt went to Washington in 1979, Jackie went with him. But she didn't stay long. The pressures were intense on both. She had been diagnosed with uterine cancer the year before and was undergoing treatment. The couple tried counseling, but separated. Gingrich has said they discussed divorce for 11 years, but Jackie insisted on trying to save the marriage.

Over the years, a body of lore has been compiled about the marriage and what broke it. Foes fond of belittling "family values" run for favorite stories: Gingrich is said to have told a friend that Jackie wasn't young enough or pretty enough to be the wife of a president. He denies those comments and accuses reporters of dredging up the same tired material. "It's always the same three or four disgruntled former aides who spout this stuff," he says.

When asked why his marriage ended, Gingrich attempts to be honest while maintaining his own privacy. He never has denied that he broke his marriage vows. In fact, he has almost confirmed it in many forums. "I'm human," he'll say, "and all human beings sin."

The left-wing magazine, *Mother Jones*, published a memorable profile of him in 1984, copies of which still are passed out in some offices in the Georgia Capitol. The question was put to him: Were the values he lived the same ones he spoke?

"No. In fact I think they were sufficiently inconsistent that at one point in 1979 and 1980, I began to quit saying them in public. One of the reasons I ended up getting a divorce was that if I was disintegrating enough as a person that I could not say those things, then I needed to get my life straight, not quit saying them. And I think that literally was the crisis I came to. I guess I look back on it a little bit like somebody who's in

Alcoholics Anonymous. It was a very, very bad period of my life, and it had been getting steadily worse. I ultimately wound up at a point where probably suicide or going insane or divorce were the last three options."

The fires were fueled in 1981, when just a few months after his divorce, Gingrich married Marianne Ginther. She was a clerk for the U.S. Secret Service and 15 years younger than Jackie. A body of stories developed that is still circulating today concerning alleged affairs with unnamed women. The tabloid program "Hard Copy" has devoted several reports to the allegations. Gingrich has attempted to draw a reasonable fence around his personal life, but the tales never seem to die. One story dominates all the others.

THE HOSPITAL VISIT ▪ In 1980, Jackie Gingrich underwent cancer surgery. Newt and his daughters went to visit. As it was portrayed in a campaign commercial in 1992, Newt "delivered divorce papers to his wife the day after her cancer operation."

The *Washington Post* reports "he pulled out a legal pad and began to discuss details of the divorce, according to accounts Jackie Gingrich confirmed in published interviews."

Gingrich and his daughters deny that divorce papers were served. "My daughters were in that hospital room," he said just after the '94 elections. "I didn't walk in there to deliver papers, I went to take my daughters for a visit. Neither of them remembers anything like that, though in a divorce the subject comes up at times like that."

Jackie Gingrich told the *Atlanta Journal,* "The girls came up and said, 'Daddy's downstairs and wants to come up.' I said sure. He was all business, going over the specifics with me in bed. It was not a pretty scene."

The issue has made for campaign fodder for years. Jackie Gingrich has given no interviews since her former husband became Speaker, but her pastor, the Rev. Brantley Harwell, has told stories of how church members took up a collection to help Jackie pay basic household bills for herself and her daughters during the separation. In 1993, Jackie went to court contending that Newt had failed to keep up payments on a life insurance policy. In recognition of his higher salary, he later increased his alimony payment to her to $1,300 a month. She, in turn, promised not to take him back to court.

The divorce, so bitter and so publicized, had one unintended effect: The published details of Gingrich's life revealed a congressman with simple tastes, modest assets, and no inclination to use the office to acquire wealth. In court documents, he listed his expenses for food and dry cleaning at $400 a month. The divorce documents, used by his foes and featured on tabloid television, have embarrassed Gingrich, but he never has become like a Sen. Herman Talmadge, whose divorce revealed him to be a man with a taste for alcohol whose coat pockets were stuffed with campaign cash.

A ROOKIE ON CAPITOL HILL ▪ Back in Washington, the Republican Party had to be reinvented. The messages that would be delivered in Renewing American Civilization were being discussed among a small cadre of Republicans as far back as 1980. They were described in David Broder's *Changing of the Guard*, a book by the columnist that profiled the next generation of political leaders in both parties. Broder's quotes from Gingrich could have been recorded in 1974, 1980, or 1994. "'I am a Republican, but I think the greatest failure of the last 20 years has been the Republican Party, not the Democratic Party. The Democratic Party has attempted to do what the governing party should do—govern. But it failed. And when it failed, there was nobody there to take up the burden. And I think that in order for this civilization to survive, at least as a free society, we've got to have a more rigorous and cohesive sense of an alternative party.'"

Gingrich told Broder how that alternative should operate. The ideas were another signpost with which to mark the young congressman as a counterrevolutionary. His goal was to lead the GOP back to its heyday, the period from 1856 to 1912 when it was the party of economic growth and the industrialization of America (the "Second Wave"). "'That was the party that created the land-grant colleges and built the transcontinental railroad. It had a vision which it was willing to impose upon the society.'"

Few were listening to Professor Gingrich back then; his message was slightly at odds with the conventional wisdom of the 1980 election. To Ronald Reagan, government was the enemy. To Newt Gingrich, government must be part of the "spirit of invention and discovery."

With Republicans in charge of the Senate and so many moderately conservative Democrats in the House, the liberal wing of the Democratic Party seemed tamed. Reagan's tax cuts, defense buildup, and reductions in spending growth were enacted, easing the incentive for voters to worry too much about the liberal threat.

Gingrich worried, though, for he was in the minority in the House. Although the Reagan landslide led some Democrats to tag along, Gingrich could see that traditional party loyalties would be in evidence again as the 1982 elections approached. His strategy was to paint the Democrats as corrupt elitists, arrogant from years of power, beholden to Big Labor, radical special interests, and big-city machines.

In Rep. Charles Diggs, a Michigan Democrat, he found just the target to make his point. In his first year in the House, Gingrich set out after Diggs, who was accused of diverting funds from his congressional payroll for personal use. He kept the heat on the Democrat, pressuring the House Ethics Committee to censure him and threatening a vote to expel him. Diggs later resigned and went to prison. Measured against the bigger fish Gingrich was later to fry, Diggs now appears something of a minnow.

Many congressmen, particularly in their early years in office, are loath to hold too high a national profile for fear of offending the voters at home. Gingrich had some leeway, as he drew a series of lackluster Democratic opponents. Dock Davis in 1980, Jim Wood in 1982, and Gerald Johnson in 1984 couldn't dent him. Each time, he raised two and three times as much money as his opponents. The Gingrich machine was taking shape, with enthusiastic volunteers, a nose for press coverage, and a Newt trademark: the challenge to debate. Few speak as quickly as the Speaker. Few challengers are as grounded in the issues as incumbents.

In 1986, for instance, the Clayton County administrator, Crandle Bray, was Gingrich's opponent. The *Atlanta Constitution* pumped him up with press steroids, making him appear be the perfect candidate to oppose the "Newtron" or "the congressman from outer space." Gingrich quickly challenged him to debate. In their first encounter, for Atlanta radio station WGST, the format called for each candidate to ask his opponent a question. Gingrich went first, noting that Bray was calling himself a conservative Democrat.

"For whom did you vote for president in 1984?" he asked. Bray ducked the question. I was to be the first questioner, so I pursued it. Bray finally admitted he had voted for his party's nominee, Walter Mondale, an unpopular candidate in the South. The 1986 campaign in the Sixth Congressional District of Georgia ended right there. The candidates debated many more times, but Bray was dead in the water.

THE BIRTH OF OPPORTUNITY ■ With no serious opposition at home, Gingrich had the decade from 1978 to 1988 to worry about national issues and the positioning of the Republican Party. His staff excelled at constituent services, and he was a quick study on local issues requiring his attention. But after his first term, Washington was his focus.

Following the 1982 congressional elections, the *New York Times* began an editorial by saying "The stench of failure hangs over the Reagan presidency." A recession was underway. The Republican minority in the House was hit hard, losing 26 seats and moving in reverse, even as Reagan was rebounding.

Some trace the idea for the Conservative Opportunity Society to a meeting Gingrich had in 1982 with former President Nixon about the need for a more idea-oriented party.

"Marianne and I went to see Dick Nixon late in '82," Gingrich told me. "He said, 'You can't change the House yourself. You have to go back and form a group.' He said, 'The House Republicans have always been boring. Hell, they were boring when I was in the House. They're not used to having ideas and they're not used to thinking that ideas matter.' He said we ought to meet each month for dinner. I thought his point was right, but his structure was wrong. But you could say that the idea for the COS came from Nixon. He was responsible for a great deal of political change in this country."

The idea had been germinating well before Nixon offered his advice. Gingrich had spent four years seeing his fellow Republicans in the House react instead of act. Jack Kemp had been there, but it took the election of Ronald Reagan to carry out his ideas. In Gingrich's view there were too few Kemps. Newt reached out first to Rep. Vin Weber of Minnesota. Together they recruited Robert Walker of Pennsylvania, Judd Gregg of New Hampshire, Dan Coats of Indiana, Connie Mack of Florida, Joe Barton of Texas, and Dan Lungren and Duncan Hunter of California. The group met weekly and planned.

"Trent Lott was the godfather," Gingrich recalls. "He hosted a weekly luncheon. Everybody but Michel was invited, on the grounds that he wouldn't have tolerated it. Kemp was there, but he wasn't a member. He was too big. Dick Cheney came. I was the senior planner. I didn't have any thoughts about being in the leadership. I thought it would be five or six years before that would happen and, when it did, Cheney or Lott would be the Republican leader and I'd be the senior planner."

In a way, Professor Gingrich was back in the classroom, teaching his colleagues what he likes to call the long-wave theory of politics. For all of his apparent energy and seemingly bull-like charges in the public arena, he is a patient politician. And he isn't averse to remembering Lenin's notion of one step backward to achieve two steps forward.

Those who argue that Gingrich is inconsistent or a slave to pollsters and public opinion should note the 1983 Conservative Opportunity Society manifesto. As outlined in a conference in Baltimore to signal the arrival of the COS, it is remarkable for its consistency with 1995's Renewing American Civilization lectures. In both is the jab at those who won't change. "If Thomas Edison invented the light bulb today," Gingrich has been saying for at least 18 years, "Dan Rather would report 'The candle-making industry was threatened today.'"

In both are the quotes from the *Girl Scout Handbook*, Peter Drucker's *The Effective Executive*, Alvin Toffler's *Third Wave*, John Naisbitt's *Megatrends*, and James Madison and George Washington. Gingrich relies on futurists and management theorists to explain his belief that the welfare state is outmoded. In 1983, he offered prescient warnings of what government was to become:

"While Ronald Reagan has slowed down the liberal welfare state, he has not fundamentally changed it. He has, in fact, slowed down the rate of tax increases, slowed down the rate of bureaucracy, slowed down the rate of inflation, but in not a single case have we fundamentally left that crossroads."

Gingrich was more than bold, what with President Reagan enjoying enormous popularity. (He was soon to win a landslide reelection.)

"The fact is that President Reagan has lost control of the national agenda. Fighting deficits is becoming a code term for new tax increases. Concern over education is becoming a slogan for more federal spending. The Medicare crisis will probably lead to a new commission proposing new taxes. And the list goes on and on."

Gingrich and company went to work on how to set a new agenda. After the Baltimore conference, the Conservative Opportunity Society outlined nine issues for the coming Congress, including a balanced budget amendment to the Constitution, a line-item veto for the president, deeper tax cuts, welfare reform, and tougher anti-crime measures. In essence, it was the Contract With America 12 years in advance.

"We [in the Conservative Opportunity Society] had to have ideas larger than the other side had objections," he recalls.

Those ideas were tested in polls and became known as "65 percent issues" for their public support. (Gingrich notes that no item in 1994's Contract With America enjoyed less than 60 percent public support.) Despite the polls, however, the public did not appear ready yet for much of the COS agenda. The Reagan tax cuts were still fresh, and the federal deficit was dominating the public debate.

THE CHEAP HAWKS ■ Gingrich went around the House leadership to found the Congressional Space Caucus and, with Sen. Gary Hart of Colorado, the Military Reform Caucus.

Each would garner him headlines, though the Space Caucus more often resulted in jibes about his notion of 21st-century vacations in space. The Military Reform Caucus came at a time when the huge Reagan defense buildup was under assault. Pentagon procurement scandals were prompting stories about $600 ashtrays and $1,200 toilet seats.

Hart and Gingrich developed the "cheap hawk solution." In their view the nuclear age required a quick-response, mobile military. In many situations, such a force could be as effective as the Navy, with its expensive aircraft carriers, and the Army, with its huge, heavily armed divisions. The congressman began a practice he continues today, visiting military installations and lecturing at war colleges. Gingrich allied himself with the analysts who were developing the fast-attack tenets of maneuver warfare called the AirLand Battle Doctrine. That doctrine was developed at Fort Benning, while Newt was a kid and his dad was serving there. The "cheap hawk solution" became an arrow in the Reagan quiver, as it staved off Democratic attempts to cut the Pentagon budget. The idea faded as more drastic defense cuts followed the end of the Cold War, but it was being touted again by Gingrich after he became Speaker. "Don't try to reform the current system," he said of Pentagon procurement early in 1995. "It is hopeless. It is impossible." The Speaker views many current Pentagon policies as part of the antiquated industrial age. He is nudging the Joint Chiefs of Staff to move the military to the information age, with smart bombs delivered by pilotless drones and troops equipped with personal communications devices for command and control.

In the early 1980s, Gingrich took some positions that separated him from most of the right wing—old and new. He voted for the Alaska Lands Act and he called for the resignation of Interior Secretary James Watt, a popular figure with Reagan conservatives. Years later, he would cosponsor the Endangered Species Act, no favorite of the Republican right, and the Clean Air Act. Most of his early supporters from the environmental movement long ago gave up on him, but among Republicans, he remains a bona fide conservationist. Newt argues that he has been true to his original beliefs, while the "greens" have moved in a radical direction, toward the taking of private property without adequate compensation. Gingrich is clear in what he wants, as he made plain in a recent interview:

"We're going to try to write one [an Endangered Species Act] that's economically rational, scientifically sound, and that protects species. The core question is how do you manage the planet? You're the dominant species, and you can screw it up. The problem now is that the environmental movement is dominated by lawyers and bureaucrats, and it's a front for anti-free-enterprisers who can't say what they really believe. They use protecting species as a device to stop development. The question is, do you spend $300 million to protect one species or do you spend that money to protect 30 species?"

Two votes stood out at home in racially charged Georgia, reminding voters of the progressive reformer who began to campaign in 1974. Gingrich, very much at home in Atlanta and anxious to end the racial polarization of the two parties, voted to create a national holiday for Dr. Martin Luther King, Jr. He also broke with Reagan over South Africa, voting to impose economic sanctions in the effort to force the apartheid government to admit blacks to the political process. His friend, Steve Hanser, the historian, calls it the toughest vote Gingrich ever cast.

Still, it was for confrontation that the young congressman

was best known. As he says, it is inevitable, blunt, and direct. And in order to replace, Gingrich is fond of saying, one must first destroy. He had succeeded in forcing the ouster of Charles Diggs, a convicted felon, from Congress. He had taken the lead in disciplinary action against Representatives Gerry Studds of Massachusetts and Daniel Crane for having sexual relations with teenaged pages (Studds with a boy, Crane with a girl). "There is a thin line between civilization and chaos," he said of authority figures exploiting young people in their charge.

Those cases, however, didn't point to systemic Democratic corruption. Crane was a Republican, after all. Gingrich was looking for bigger game. His targets wouldn't present themselves until he found his methods, and television provided the perfect opportunity.

TAKING ON THE SPEAKER ■ C-Span, the cable industry's cooperative network, had been televising Congress since the year Gingrich arrived in Washington. Congressman Bob Walker was its pioneer, tirelessly arguing before the cameras on points of parliamentary procedure. Gingrich discovered that voters were asking him if knew Walker. He understood that an overwhelming number of C-Span viewers were voters. In a memorable line to Atlanta reporters, Gingrich said, "C-Span is more real than being there."

The COS members saw a media opportunity for airing their views in the "special orders" time periods at the end of the legislative day. They delivered their speeches to a mostly empty chamber, with the camera staying tight on the speaker. They also set daily themes on which to lecture during the time before each session set aside for one-minute speeches. (In early 1995, a stream of Democrats was using the one-minute speeches to excoriate Gingrich on ethical grounds and call for an independent counsel to investigate his case.) Thus the COS members bypassed the mainstream press and went unedited into voters' living rooms. Democrats were slow to react, choosing mostly to lampoon the men speaking so vigorously to an empty chamber. But voters were watching, as Gingrich and Walker knew.

C-Span, politics, and confrontation all came together in 1984. Tempers were wearing thin in the election year. The Republicans were chafing at the Democrats' dictatorial control of the House. In particular they objected to Speaker Tip O'Neill's refusal to allow yes-or-no votes on some of the key emotional issues of the day, those "65 percent issues" such as school prayer, preferring to keep such items bottled up in committee or doomed by procedural votes easily explained away at home. Many such bills would no doubt have passed, repudiating the House's liberal leadership. And the conservatives simmered still over O'Neill's refusal in 1983 to allow any debate or amendments to the Equal Rights Amendment to the Constitution.

The COS members enthusiastically supported U.S. aid for the contra rebels fighting the Sandinistas, the Marxists in control of the government of Nicaragua. To Reagan and the COS, the contras were freedom fighters. To most Democrats, they were thugs. Typical was the thinking of one of Gingrich's colleagues, Wyche Fowler, a liberal Democrat from Atlanta. Fowler argued that the Sandinistas threatened no one. "They were armed only with broomsticks," he said. "And if they're Marxists, they're Groucho Marxists."

In May, a group of House Democrats, including Majority Leader Jim Wright of Texas, wrote what became known as the "Dear Commandante" letter to Daniel Ortega, the Sandinista leader, attempting to negotiate a peace. Ortega embarrassed them in short order by heading off to Moscow for a dollop of Soviet aid and support. Gingrich rose on the floor of the House to attack the letter writers. He said they were "blind to communism" and had a defeatist view of America's role in the world. A few days later, the affable O'Neill lost his cool before the full chamber and the cameras. He accused Gingrich of McCarthyite tactics and of questioning the patriotism of the Democrats.

"You deliberately stood in the well before an empty House and challenged these people and you challenged their Americanism. It's the lowest thing I've ever seen in my 32 years in Congress."

Rep. Trent Lott of Mississippi was quick to react, demanding that O'Neill's words be "taken down," stricken from the record on the grounds that personal attacks are barred on the floor. It was a rare rebuke. For his part, O'Neill misjudged his foes. He called them "an asset to the Democratic Party" and said they turned off the American people. But for Gingrich, it was his first moment in the national sun. Back in Georgia, where Tip O'Neill was about as popular as Walter Mondale and Geraldine Ferraro, Gingrich's 1984 opponent, Gerald Johnson, was defeated even before he started the fall campaign.

TACTICAL ADVANTAGES ▪ The COS fought a few other battles as well. To support Reagan in his efforts to pass legislation permitting school prayer, they held an all-night vigil session on the subject. They got publicity for their cause, but they remained frustrated by the refusal of the Democrats to allow votes on school prayer and other key issues.

Gingrich, Vin Weber, and Bob Walker—O'Neill had dubbed them the "Three Stooges"—had seen Reagan's six initiatives for the 1984 Congress bottled up by Democrats. One of them was the equal access bill, a measure allowing religious and other groups from outside school systems to use high-school facilities. It was a fallback from school prayer.

The "Stooges" had been harassing the leadership with "calendar Wednesdays," a procedural device that allows a committee chairman to call up a bill that the Speaker or Rules Committee chairman has been blocking. The three men hoped to force the Democrats to vote against any of the "hot" social issues. No chairman had taken up their cause, however. One day, Gingrich found himself walking off the floor with Carl Perkins, the venerable Kentuckian who chaired the Education and Labor Committee. Perkins told the younger man that he remembered the "calendar Wednesday" tactic with fondness, for it was the means by which civil rights measures were brought to the floor over the objections of Southern segregationists in the 1940s. Speaker Sam Rayburn was often foiled by it.

Perkins, it so happened, liked the equal access bill and agreed with Gingrich to bring it up on a "calendar Wednesday." His move so provoked O'Neill that the two aging colleagues fell into a shouting match, with Perkins calling O'Neill's actions "unlawful." But Perkins prevailed on the rule, and the bill was passed 337 to 77, allowing groups to pray in school, but after school.

COMING-OUT PARTY FOR A RISING STAR ■ By August and the 1984 Republican National Convention in Dallas, Gingrich was a hot property. He had rushed his book, *Window of Opportunity*, into print to be able to distribute it at the convention, and he had political consultant Eddie Mahe on hand to help him reach a broader audience. Ronald Reagan was to speak of an "opportunity society" in his 1985 State of the Union address. On the day before the convention opened, Gingrich was covered in at least six major Sunday newspapers. He and his book were featured in *The New Republic*. He was a star at a humdrum convention at which Reagan's renomination was assured. At one point, Gingrich turned down an interview with Dan Rather on CBS to do one with C-Span. His reasoning was consistent: "I owe C-Span. I don't owe CBS."

On convention evening, I sat with him in a hotel lobby surrounded by his constituents, one of whom was wearing a Reagan button that played the National Anthem over and over. The firebrand wasn't scheduled to address the convention. "There's a Nixonian level of control over this convention," Gingrich muttered, "that's just plain silly. A party of ideas has to have speeches long enough to have ideas in them."

He sounded a warning for the future that amazed me, considering the popularity Ronald Reagan was enjoying.

"If the national press calls you anything at this stage, it's a victory. At least the press recognizes how the COS controlled the platform. We're setting the framework on which all presidential candidates in the GOP will run in 1988. When Reagan and his staff think through the State of the Union address and their agenda for a second term, they better be thinking about what we believe, or they'll face a revolution in their own party."

Gingrich's revolt against his own party wouldn't come until George Bush was president. Reagan's strength—and conservatism—was beyond even Newt's reach. Besides, first for Gingrich was the little matter of a real assault on the Democratic Party.

An intramural skirmish in Congress at the beginning of Reagan's second term helped Gingrich and the COS bring allies to their cause. After a tense race in Indiana's Eighth Congressional District, the Republican Richard McIntyre was certified the winner by 34 votes. When Congress convened, the Democrats refused to seat him. After a long legal battle and a task force investigation, the full House voted along party lines to seat Frank McCloskey, the incumbent Democrat. That prompted a walkout by the entire Republican caucus, both old bulls and young turks, down the steps of the Capitol in protest.

The event raised Gingrich's credibility by driving home his point that going along to get along would never work. Many moderate Republicans came to believe that arrogance was corrupting the traditions of the House. Those who thought Gingrich guilty of overblown speechmaking were beginning to agree with an observation he made in 1984:

"Democrats would go on the floor to kick Republicans and show their contempt. The ranking Republicans would say how grateful they were to work with the chairman, when he had 70 staff people and they had three. It was the whole psychology of master and servant."

REFINING THE CONSERVATIVE AGENDA ∎
For much of 1985, Gingrich lowered his profile, seeing if he could alter his style to become an insider and leader of more troops. The COS, after all, numbered just 40 members. In 1986, Gingrich went back to attacking the welfare state, trying out ideas to build a conservative majority and, incidentally, running for reelection.

He kept his focus on national affairs, bolstered by the Almanac of American Politics, which named him one of the 26 most influential members of the House. His standard speech that year offered a six-point prescription: 1) Base the welfare system on work; 2) expand day care—private and public—to accommodate welfare mothers; 3) make "mutual trade"—neither free trade nor protectionism—the country's goal (this was an attempt to reconcile two wings of his party); 4) privatize many government services, starting with the National Aeronautics and Space Administration; 5) reform the Pentagon, with a move away from all-volunteer standing forces to more emphasis on reserves and the National Guard; and, following the Senate's lead, 6) curb cost-of-living increases in social programs such as Social Security.

At first, his attention to national issues didn't seem to have consequences at home. But a future opponent, Dave Worley, was taking notes, especially on Gingrich's many suggestions about Social Security. When the young Harvard-trained lawyer faced Gingrich in 1988, he showed some skill, but lost by 17 percentage points. Gingrich had talked several years before about plans to privatize the Social Security system, offering workers the option of expanded Individual Retirement Accounts. Such ideas had been flowing from conservative and libertarian think tanks for years and never had a chance of passage, but in the 1988 campaign, Worley seized upon Gingrich's suggestions and harped on them at every stop. It's not for nothing that Social Security is called "the third rail of American politics": Politicians who touch it are likely to get a shock. The attacks forced Gingrich into intensive damage control, along with some uncharacteristic whining about Worley.

"He is the least ethical candidate I've ever had to run against," said Gingrich of Worley's warnings on Social Security. "He's a Harvard magna cum laude graduate; he's very smart, proof that IQ and honor are not always the same thing. This man is so despicable and so desperate to be a congressman that he is deliberately scaring 80- and 90-year-old people with what he knows is a lie."

THE ETHICAL ASSAULT ▪ While he was disposing of Worley in the 1988 campaign, Gingrich continued the attacks he had begun the year before on his biggest Democratic target yet. Against the advice of most political advisers, he had begun a spirited campaign to undermine the new House Speaker, Jim Wright of Texas. He called Wright "the least ethical Speaker in this century." On this one, Gingrich was out there by himself. His assault discomfited Robert Michel, the House minority leader, and many COS members.

Gingrich put staff to work investigating the Speaker and pushed his case to the press, on the floor, and around the nation. He got the break he needed when the *Washington Post* disclosed that Wright had an unusual publishing arrangement for his book, *Reflections of a Public Man*. The collection of his speeches was published by a top aide and earned the Speaker a 55 percent royalty, far more than the standard 15 percent. Worse, Wright's people were selling it to lobbying groups and union gatherings in bulk, allowing him to earn money from speaking engagements well above the limits imposed on speaking fees for House members. As Gingrich had predicted, the House Ethics Committee was moved to action when Common Cause, the self-styled citizen's lobbying group, called for an investigation.

Frederick Allen, then the political editor of the *Atlanta Constitution*, put it well. "Any time the story line is books, bulk sales and Teamsters Union, all in the same sentence, you've got a problem."

Wright accused Gingrich and his allies of "mindless cannibalism," but his counterattack was doomed. The House Ethics Committee found much more than the book deal: 69 alleged violations of House rules, including a sham company that provided for Wright's wife and unreported gifts from people with an interest in legislation. Wright resigned in 1989.

The Speaker's fall meant several things to Gingrich and the Republicans. First, Gingrich was the undisputed leader of the COS. He had given meaning to one of his favored maxims, the kind first put in the shoeboxes of his teenaged years, then on

Post-it Notes, and recently into a laptop computer: "Real leadership is letting others invest their fears in your courage."

More important, stripping the bark from Wright helped Gingrich's cause beyond Wright's personal disgrace. The Texas congressman's fall also cut away one of the last layers of pretense from Southern representatives who claimed at home to be moderate or conservative, but voted in Washington with their party's liberal wing. Wright had circumvented the White House and State Department by trying to negotiate with a Marxist government in Nicaragua. He opposed tax cuts and endorsed the Great Society's social programs. He was Tip O'Neill with a Texas twang. Gingrich's strategy of attacking the enemy's ideology by spotlighting its corruption had begun to pay off. And his grand vision was beginning to look less like a young man's fancy and more like something that strategy, tactics, and projects could achieve.

A RUN FOR THE TOP ▪ Following Wright's resignation came a surprise. After John Tower was rejected as President Bush's nominee for Secretary of Defense, the president nominated House Minority Whip Dick Cheney, the calm, collected Wyoming congressman. Cheney's selection would open up the number-two Republican leadership position in the House.

There was an unusual leadership vacuum on the Republican side. Trent Lott, a previous whip and COS leader, had gone on to the U.S. Senate. Jack Kemp had left to run for president. Now Cheney was gone. To the astonishment of many in Washington and Georgia, Gingrich decided to run. The job of whip, named for its chief responsibility of counting and rounding up votes, didn't seem the sort of detail work Gingrich would like. The COS group of Walker and others went to work on their Republican colleagues. Newt's opponent was Edward Madigan of Illinois, later to be named Secretary of Agriculture. Republican traditions in place since the party became a minority in 1954 suggested that Madigan's election would be a foregone conclusion: He was the choice of Minority Leader Bob Michel, he was mildly conservative, and he was well liked.

For the first time, Gingrich showed the press and his Democratic critics that his skills went beyond warlike strategies and bombastic speeches. He went directly to the moderate Republicans who were expected to oppose him. At the time, their misery over their minority status was so profound that they gave Gingrich a hearing. Their president was in the White House but in their own House they were an afterthought. In Gingrich they saw a bright man with ideas not too far afield from theirs who could rally their party. Something Gingrich told the *Atlanta Journal* in 1985 summed up the plight of the minority party.

"The House is a place where for years liberal Democrats mugged Republicans randomly. The Republicans' job was to hand over their wallet and be grateful that was all they wanted. Now, we're sort of like the guy on the New York subway who shot back. We look confrontational because when we get mugged, we fight back."

Gingrich had been building bridges to the moderate group of Republicans for years. With the help of Representatives Nancy Johnson of Connecticut and Steve Gunderson of Wisconsin, he won their support and defeated Madigan in a close vote, 87–85. The White House was edgy, senior Republicans nervous, and Democrats ecstatic, for President Bush needed a bipartisan approach to work with a Democratic Congress. Gingrich, many in both parties thought, would be a large crowbar in those wheels.

AT HOME, IGNORED ■ In those years, Gingrich intensified the work habits that amaze his friends. His 6 A.M. walks near the Capitol drew regular press companions. He called associates early in the morning and late at night. He came home to his district for nonstop town hall meetings and political gatherings. It all took a toll on his marriage.

Marianne Gingrich is a pleasant, lively woman, but not a political animal. She is bright and shares her husband's capacity for strategic thinking. But while Newt only rarely unwinds, preferring his practice of managing his days in 15-minute increments, Marianne is able to enjoy herself in a lighthearted way. She jokes and giggles around the periphery of political events and has a talent for deflating the pompous, her husband included. But Marianne hails from a small town in Ohio, and Washington has never appealed to her. She has managed, somehow, to keep up a cheerful public face. In 1988, at the Republican Convention in New Orleans, gossip about the Gingrich marriage was flying. It almost eclipsed a nasty fight between regular Republicans in the Georgia delegation and insurgents from the religious right. Since then, her leaving him or him leaving her has been the Republican rumor du jour.

Newt and Marianne have been surprisingly open about their problems. In a *Washington Post* profile in 1989, Newt's remarks seemed of the Phil Donahue variety.

"You talk about crying," he said. "The spring of 1988, I spent a fair length of time trying to come to grips with who I was and the habits I had and what they did to people that I truly loved. I really spent a period of time where, I suspect, I cried three or four times a week. I read *Men Who Hate Women and the Women Who Love Them* and I found frightening pieces that related..."

Marianne revealed that the marriage had been "off and on" for some time, seeming to confirm rumors they had split up at least once. In a comment that angered many women for its appeareance of cold-hearted calculation, Newt said he believed the marriage had a "53-47" chance of surviving. As of 1995, his handicapping was on the money; the marriage is working. As his friend Steve Hanser noted in the spring, "They've been married 14 years, something a lot of folks can't say. And they've worked at it."

PAYBACK TIME IN GEORGIA ▪ From the time Gingrich began his fight against Jim Wright, the Sixth District of Georgia seemed far away from the congressman's priorities. His national agenda appeared to come first. In August of 1989, Gingrich went off for 18 days to the mountains of Colorado to develop the strategy to go with his vision of a conservative majority. The end of the Cold War removed a key sheet of the Republican armor that had allowed the party to dominate presidential politics since 1968. The GOP had been the party of strong defense. In many ways, containment of communism was its touchstone. Now the party needed a domestic agenda and strategy to achieve its majority.

Gingrich stayed in a cabin at Crested Butte, the resort developed by Howard "Bo" Callaway, a pioneer Georgia Republican and stalwart of GOPAC, the political action committee Gingrich was turning into a campaign think tank, academy, and central bank. The stay in the mountains, without electricity or a phone, was another building block toward the Contract With America. Gingrich invited in allies and experts, and came away with a focus on a domestic agenda that would stand up into 1994.

Gingrich was preoccupied. He had his marital difficulties and his broader new responsiblities as Minority Whip. In addition, his big win over Dave Worley in 1988 seemed to embolden him. He signed on to a bipartisan agreement granting Congress a whopping 35-percent pay raise over two years. In one sense it was a good government measure because it carried with it lower limits on speaking fees, too often thinly disguised payoffs or excuses for luxurious vacations courtesy of special interests. But Americans howled, seeing the pay raise as a prime example of Washington arrogance. The issue marked the emergence of talk radio as a recognized political force—sometimes conservative, mainly populist.

As the 1990 election neared, Gingrich seemed unaware of the anger among his constituents and even fellow Republicans. He had created a monster that was about to jump out of its cage. The hammering at official corruption had harmed the image of the House. The pay raise made congressmen seem like a band of embezzlers. And still to come was the scandal of the House Bank.

In Georgia, Worley, Gingrich's Democratic opponent, was running hard in his rematch, capitalizing on a recession. To add to the disaffection at home, Gingrich spent much of 1990 first working with the White House on a budget deal with the Democrats, then breaking with President Bush over a tax increase in a most dramatic manner at the eleventh hour. The congressman's long-range vision was leaving him unable to see the world right in front of his nose. In the 1990 campaign, Dave Worley almost turned Gingrich into Jack Flynt, the out-of-touch veteran whom Gingrich ran into retirement in 1978.

Worley had little money. The Democratic Congressional Campaign Committee wanted to beat "Newtron," but backed away from contributing the funds necessary for a targeted campaign when Worley made congressional pay raises a central issue of the campaign. To obtain a measure of political protection, both parties had agreed to try to prevent candidates from attacking incumbents who voted for the pay raise. The Democrats missed a golden opportunity to defeat the future Speaker. Worley had to work harder. He painted Gingrich as out of touch, more interested in national television appearances than in the people of Georgia. In fact, Gingrich *was* out of touch. His campaign was run from Washington by the national strategist, Joe Gaylord. To Gaylord, Georgia voters, press, and politicians were push pins on a map of a remote territory.

Worley played to the anger of several constituent groups. He set up limousines along busy commuter routes to illustrate his charge that Newt had "gone Washington," with limo and chauffeur. Gingrich did use a Lincoln Town Car and security officer provided him as GOP Whip. The congressional pay raise was kerosene on a growing fire.

The recession was hitting hard in the suburbs south of Atlanta. Eastern Airlines employees went on strike against the cost-cutting tactics of Frank Lorenzo. They wanted federal intervention and historically were suspicious of Republicans on labor-management issues. The strike provided Worley 6,000 enraged volunteers with time on their hands and the sympathies of close to 20,000 other aviation workers employed at Hartsfield International Airport. Nearby residents also were concerned about plans to add a fifth runway to Hartsfield, endangering close-in communities.

Everywhere Gingrich campaigned, strikers made their voices heard. Gingrich angered them further by refusing to join a House effort to convince President Bush to convene an emergency board to end the strike. The Eastern strike would lead to the demise of the company and the loss of thousands of jobs. Gingrich believed the airline couldn't be saved. In hindsight, he probably was right, strike or no strike. But in the heat of a campaign, the appearance of inaction by the congressman hurt him.

Worley attacked on other fronts. He pored over Gingrich's records in search of ethical improprieties. He charged, for instance, that the financing of Gingrich's first novel by some wealthy investors while he was teaching at West Georgia College wasn't an investment in a potential bestseller, but a scheme to improperly funnel money to the candidate. He tried to link contributions from savings and loan operators to Congress's failure to prevent the national collapse of the industry. Worley relied heavily on direct mail. The front of one piece said, "One peach for you." Its flipside read, "And $35,000 for the congressman."

On election night, first reports showed Gingrich trailing. Cheers went up in the Democrat-dominated Georgia state capitol and, some press accounts claimed, in the office of House Republican leader Robert Michel. In the wee hours of the morning, Gingrich appeared to have squeaked by, although a recount was in the offing. When all was said and done, the number-two Republican in the Congress had won by 970 votes over an opponent who failed to broadcast a single television commercial.

When it was over, Gingrich again looked inside himself. Aware he had neglected bread-and-butter issues, he referred to abstract theory as "college professor stuff." And in a post-mortem, he said to me, "Ideas have consequences, but they're better with a smile."

His difficulties balancing a national vision with the meat-and-potatoes Georgia voters weren't over. But they were put aside for a while. Gingrich's experience breaking with Bush on the budget deal and tax increase had started him in the direction of his conservative majority. Ahead lay four years of planning and yet another near disaster.

CHAPTER 7

THE
CONTRACT

"What is at issue is literally not Republican or Democrat
or liberal or conservative, but the question of whether or
not our civilization will survive.

Since the election, the article which has most
accurately captured its essence is Charles Krauthammer's
column this morning in the Washington Post, which
makes the correct point that you have the most explicitly
ideologically committed House Republican Party in
modern history. That we held an event on September 27
on the Capitol steps that over 300 members or candidates
signed up for. That we told the country in a full-page ad
in TV Guide where we were going and the direction we
would take. That President Clinton and Tony Coehlo
took up the challenge. That the Democratic National
Committee ran $2 million of ads attacking the Contract
With America. That the president personally attacked the
Contract virtually everywhere he went. And in the end
there was the most shattering one-sided Republican
victory since 1946.

Since then, there's been an enormous effort by the
Washington elite to avoid the reality that this lesson was
actually about some fairly big ideas. Which direction do
you want to go in? And that those who argued for
counterculture values, bigger government, redistribu-
tionist economics, and bureaucracies deciding how you
should spend your money, were on the losing end in
virtually every part of the country.

It's very hard for the Washington elite to come to grips

with the reality that there's now a national Republican
Party. That's the biggest single message of this election.
That for the first time in history, the Civil War, in effect,
is over, and Republicans were able to run everywhere
simultaneously. And, standing on Ronald Reagan's
shoulders, the Republican Party now has enough recruits
and enough resources and enough leaders to actually be
capable of running everywhere.

This was clearly a historic election which clearly had a
mandate. And that's outside the Washington elite's view,
and they don't want to believe that because it's not the
mandate they wanted.

I want to draw a distinction between two words,
because we're going to get into a lot of confusion at the
vision level about these two words. I am very prepared to
cooperate with the Clinton administration. I am not
prepared to compromise. The two words are very
different.

On everything on which we can find agreement, I will
cooperate. On those things which are at the core of our
philosophy, and on those things where we believe we
represent the vast majority of Americans, there will be no
compromise. So let me draw the distinction: Cooperation,
yes. Compromise, no.

I, frankly, became more radical all fall. I realized as I
would talk to audiences—I was in 127 districts in the last
two years—and I realized as I would talk to audiences
that there was an enormous danger that they were going
to say, 'Terrific speech, let's elect Gingrich Speaker, let's
elect our local candidate to the House, they'll do the job.'

And let me tell all of you flatly, the long experiment in
professional politicians and professional government is
over, and it failed. You cannot hire a teacher to teach
your child and walk off and then blame the teacher. You
cannot hire a policeman to protect your neighborhood
and then walk off and blame police. You cannot hire a
public health service to protect your health and then walk
off and blame the public health service.

This means my challenge to the American people is simple. You really want to reduce power in Washington? You have to be willing to take more responsibility back home. You really want to reduce the bureaucracy of the welfare state? You have to accept greater responsibility back home. We are going to have to be partners.

The event on September 27 was designed as a subset of these big principles. The Capitol steps event basically said, look, we are a team, we are going to go in a dramatically different direction, we're going to give you eight reforms on the opening day, starting with the Shays Act, which will apply to Congress every law it applies to the rest of the country so congressmen will learn all the problems they've imposed on everybody else.

We are going to cut the number of congressional staffs by a third, and we sent a letter to that effect to Speaker Tom Foley on Wednesday, frankly in order to allow the Democratic staff to know that a substantial number of them ought to be looking for jobs, because we thought that was the most decent and correct way to deal with it. We are going to cut the number of congressional committees. We are going to eliminate the current services budget and replace it with a straight-line budget, where if you have a dollar increase it counts as a dollar increase. This is the only place in the world where you can increase spending massively and it counts as a cut. And it has been a major source of the problem of dealing with the deficit because you create a linguistic barrier to honesty. And we're simply going to eliminate it.

At the end of the opening day, we will introduce the 10 bills we described in the Contract. We will read the Contract as the opening item of business every day for the first 100 days, and at the end of the first 100 days the American people, at Easter, will be able to say they saw a group of people who actually said what they were going to do and then kept their word.

Now, we don't guarantee we'll pass all 10, and it's very clear in the Contract that what—some of these are *very controversial—litigation reform, including mal-practice, product liability, and strike law firms is one item; a balanced budget amendment to the Constitution; a vote on term limits; an effective, enforceable death penalty with a one-time unified appeal; beginning the phaseout of the marriage penalty in the tax code; allowing senior citizens to earn up to $39,000 a year without penalty from Social Security; a capital gains cut and indexing.*

These are not small things, but they move in the right direction. Welfare reform, emphasizing work and family. A line-item veto, including, frankly, a line-item veto for this president, so that we as Republican conservatives are prepared to give to President Clinton a line-item veto because we think it's right for America. These are real changes. It's going to be real hard to do and it's going to take a lot of people helping.

Let me say just one last thing. If this just degenerates after an historic election back into the usual baloney of politics in Washington and pettiness in Washington, then the American people I believe will move toward a third party in a massive way. I think they are fed up with Washington, they are fed up with its games, they are fed up with petty partisanship. I don't think they mind grand partisanship, and there's a big difference. To have a profound disagreement over the direction of your country or over the principles by which your economy works, or over the manner in which your government should structure resources, that is legitimate and the American people believe in that level of debate and relish it.

The question will be over the next six months, can we reach out to the American people, can we recruit enough of them—notice I didn't say 'Republicans'—the American people.

When you hear gunshots in your nation's capital at night and you know young Americans have died needlessly, then I would suggest to you that we have every reason to have the moral courage to confront every weakness of the current structure and replace it, and if the first wave of experiments fail, to have the courage to say, 'Well, that one didn't work,' and have a second one and a third one and a fourth one. And the Monday morning we can wake up and we can look on the morning news and no young American was killed anywhere in America, and we can know that every one of them is going to a school where they're actually learning how to read, and we know that they live under a tax code where if they want to it's easy to start creating jobs and have your own business, and it's easy to start accumulating a little money to create a better future, that morning I think we can say, 'Okay, this journey has been worth it.' But until that day, it just stays politics.

We have an enormous amount of work to do. All I can promise you on the side of the House Republicans is that we're going to be open to working with everyone, that we will cooperate with anyone, and we will compromise with no one, and that's the base of where we're going and that's what we believe this election is all about."

(Newt Gingrich, remarks to the Washington Research Group Symposium, November 11, 1994)

Who knows exactly when or how the Contract With America began? Perhaps it was at the Baltimore conference of 1983 to launch the Conservative Opportunity Society. That year, Judd Gregg, now a senator from New Hampshire, sent Gingrich a memo outlining nine of the 10 points that later appeared in the Contract. Many observers credit Gingrich's 1989 sojourn in the Colorado Rockies, in which he put his thinking in order. Maybe it began at an August, 1990, lecture to the Heritage Foundation, in which Gingrich set forth his six goals for the nation and attempted to energize accommodationist Republicans.

The Speaker himself says the seed was planted in October, 1980, when Republican members of the House and Senate gathered on the steps of the U.S. Capitol with Ronald Reagan and highlighted his presidential platform. He says he tried again with his 1986 speeches suggesting six points for America's future, including Social Security reform. It was at Crested Butte in 1989, he says, that he realized "the scale of the transformation that was needed." The welfare state "must be blown up to be replaced."

Howard "Bo" Callaway, the pioneer Georgia Republican, remembers a meeting as far back as 1981 in Racine, Wisconsin, at which Gingrich laid out a 12-year plan for a conservative majority. "He was a year late," Callaway jokes. Indeed, one could ask whether Newt and his pal Jim Tilton had a battle plan way back at Baker High School when they dreamed of a Republican majority.

RESTIVE REAGANITES ▪ Wherever the origin of its philosophy lies, the boldness and audacity of the Contract can be traced to Gingrich's decision in 1990 to challenge George Bush on taxes and budget priorities. Gingrich may cite his visit as a teen to the ossuary at Verdun as his defining moment, but in political terms, challenging a sitting president of one's own party—a president standing tall in the polls— must be considered either a master stroke or political suicide.

Bush was the model of an establishment Republican. Inside Washington, he practiced the "kinder, gentler" politics he preached in his 1988 campaign. Despite his Texas business career and public embrace of the rougher hewn conservatism of the American West, he was true to his roots—a Connecticut Yankee who practiced noblesse oblige. The president could eat pork rinds and listen to country music, but he was more attuned to the Nelson Rockefeller wing of the party than the Reagan-Goldwater wing. Bush had a generational rapport with the Republican leader, Bob Michel. Each was a traditional centrist Republican. Each had served with distinction in World War II. Bush may even have seen Michel's son play basketball for Yale, Bush's alma mater.

Gingrich was a different breed. Ideas came before the art of the deal.

While Bush was serving his eight years as vice president to Ronald Reagan and awaiting his big chance, the GOP had changed. The Conservative Opportunity Society and emboldened moderates had turned to Gingrich for strategy and tactics, if not always for leadership. It isn't clear that Bush ever understood the trend. As president, he governed with the views of congressional Democrats first on his priority list. To pass legislation, Bush had to get Democrats on board. Too often, House Republican sensibilities became an afterthought.

Most of those House Republicans were Reaganites, another group the Bush White House took great pains to exclude from policy making. The younger Conservative Opportunity Society members were known derisively around the White House as "bumper-sticker conservatives." Charles Kolb, a Bush official, aptly described the situation in his 1994 book *White House Daze.*

"The fruits of this curious predilection—the need to coddle the Democratic opposition, while simultaneously ignoring or even vilifying the administration's natural GOP supporters—were abundantly present by the second year of the Bush administration."

Bush, of course, had made his famous tax pledge at the 1988 Republican convention. "Read my lips," he proclaimed, "no new taxes." Even more than foreign policy, the tax issue had united the party in the 1988 elections and highlighted the Republicans' sharp contrast with the Democratic nominee, Michael Dukakis of Massachusetts.

Bush, always more comfortable with foreign than domestic policy, seemed determined to dispose of domestic issues as painlessly as possible. The contentious young turks in the House, well aware that the Berlin Wall was down and the Soviet empire disintegrating, were focusing on domestic policy and social issues. They wanted a capital gains tax cut, enterprise zones for cities, and tax fairness for families. Bush may have promised not to raise taxes, but he had not promised to cut them.

READ MY LIPS: HIGHER TAXES ■
Gingrich's first skirmish with the White House was over
foreign policy—the president's veto of a bill that would have
allowed Chinese students to stay in the U.S. after their visas
expired. The brutal suppression of protestors in Beijing's
Tiananmen Square in 1989 had been seen in living rooms
across America. Chinese students' lives were put at risk as
soon as they returned home. Supported by Gingrich,
Republicans joined Democrats in attempting to override the
veto, and Bush administration officials began to be wary of
the gadfly from Georgia.

But the major battle came in 1990 over taxes. Bush, with
most of his attention focused on the Middle East, had been
negotiating a budget agreement with Democratic congressional leaders. Republicans were along for the ride. Bush was
about to agree to tax increases, shattering his Reagan-like
pledge and launching "lips" jokes by cynics everywhere.

The White House press office distributed a statement from
Bush in June: "It is clear to me that both the size of the deficit
problem and the need for a package that can be enacted
require all of the following: entitlement and mandatory
program reform; tax revenue increases; growth incentives;
discretionary spending reductions; orderly reductions in
defense expenditures; and budget process reform."

In *Why Americans Hate Politics*, E.J. Dionne summed up
the turnabout:

"For the Republican right, the way out of the federal
budget mess was clear: further cuts in domestic spending.
Some on the right, such as House Whip Newt Gingrich, even
called for *more* tax cuts. For Bush, however, this strategy
raised a host of problems. As a political matter, large segments
of government spending never stopped being popular—
notably social security and Medicare. Squeezing those
programs carried a very high electoral cost. And with Bush
attempting a modest leftward correction in the Republicans'
posture—mixing a bit of Modern Republicanism in with
Reagan Republicanism—he was ill-placed to slash federal
outlays. That was not the route to a 'kinder, gentler' nation."

In *White House Daze*, Charles Kolb was rougher. He spoke for most conservatives when he wrote: "With this one assertion [violating the no-tax pledge], Bush squandered not only his political capital but also his credibility. Democrats now knew for a certainty that he would compromise with them on even his most fundamental 'beliefs.'"

The Democrats played winning poker during the long negotiations held in private at Andrews Air Force Base. They stripped the political clothing from Bush, right down to his shorts. In the name of a five-year deficit reduction plan, they got the president to drop his effort to cut the capital gains tax rate and to increase the levies on gasoline, alcohol, and tobacco. It was a blow to the middle class, many of them Reagan Democrats, that would doom the Bush presidency. Public cynicism would skyrocket and voter participation would decline.

Whether Gingrich ever signed on to the compromise is a matter of dispute. Although a participant in the bipartisan budget negotiations, Gingrich was described by many participants as disengaged, reading novels and making notes, his mind elsewhere—perhaps on his principles. The congressman was in close contact with his allies in the House, assuring them that he would insist that a capital gains tax cut be the basis of any agreement and that there could be no increase in marginal income tax rates.

On the other hand, White House officials believed they had at least an unspoken agreement with Gingrich that he was on board. They ignored his break with Reagan over the 1982 tax increases and a speech by the congressman to the Heritage Foundation that called for tax cuts. In an August, 1990, interview with me and in speeches throughout his district, Gingrich had called for cutting the capital gains tax to 15 percent, easing restrictions on Individual Retirement Accounts, and tripling the income tax deduction for children.

Newt was fairly shouting about the folly of raising taxes at the onset of a recession. But the president and his staff weren't listening. Gingrich offers an inside-the-Beltway explanation for why the House staff didn't believe he was serious.

"By the standard of Washington," he says, "where I was telling the truth I was lying. Because, by the standard of Washington, the signals I was sending should have been that I would cave but this was my public cover. Since I actually meant what I was saying, I was, by the standard of Washington, being dishonest."

Gingrich now says he should have abandoned the discussions in June of 1990. By August, he says, he realized that the Democrats would force their own plan on the president. Two weeks before the president and his opponents reached an agreement, they abandoned Andrews Air Force Base and met daily at the White House. Gingrich and another tax cutter, Sen. Phil Gramm of Texas, were excluded from the talks. "It meant the president was surrounded by his enemies," Gingrich recalls.

The final break came in dramatic fashion. The closed-door negotiations wrapped up on Saturday, September, 29, 1990. A ceremony in the White House Rose Garden was set for Sunday. That day, the leadership of both parties met with Bush beforehand. Gingrich astounded his colleagues by saying he didn't believe the plan would pass and that he wouldn't support it. The president and the others went off to the Rose Garden and the television cameras, and Gingrich went home.

Administration officials were angry. Richard Darman, Bush's budget director and no favorite of conservatives, was quoted as saying Gingrich's walk from the budget talks was a "stab in the back." Gingrich told of meeting with Bush and apologizing for what had happened. "You're killing us," Gingrich quoted the president as saying, "you're just killing us."

In the end, Bush had to give even more ground to Democrats. He lost the vote on the first compromise, with 105 House Republicans siding with Gingrich and only 71 with the GOP leader, Bob Michel. With his own party split and relying on Democratic votes for passage, the president was forced to compromise even further. The top marginal income tax rate was raised to 31 percent, and higher-income families lost their personal exemptions. It was a messy, complicated episode, one that convinced few voters the deficit was truly being reduced. Kolb described the aftermath: "As a further indication of just how far the worm was turning, we now had a situation in which the Bush administration had just agreed to raising taxes, renouncing Reaganomics, and acquiescing in major domestic spending increases, while simultaneously castigating GOP members of Congress who were willing to stand up for real spending cuts, economic growth and lower taxes!"

Vice President Dan Quayle was more succinct. "All the President got," he wrote in *Standing Firm*, "was four months of agony and a broken promise that would haunt him for the rest of his presidency."

What couldn't be seen at the time was that the conservative movement was now rooted securely in the House, awaiting its majority, even if Gingrich was being called, in the words of the *New Republic*, "a flaky, reedy-voiced gadfly." Four years later, the *Washington Post* would call Gingrich's split with the president a winning strategy. "Republican Party Rift Is the Necessary Sting of Realizing the Whip's Vision," proclaimed a headline. To create a Republican majority, it was necessary to go so far as to break with a Republican president and put the spotlight on a new set of ideas. That benefit wasn't seen at the time, except perhaps in the House. In Georgia, the effect of Gingrich's break with Bush on taxes was to dislodge a few loyal Republican voters and give former Democrats another reason to vote for Dave Worley, his opponent in 1990.

A MOVE TO SAFER TERRITORY ▪ If the break with Bush over bedrock Republican principles was liberating for Gingrich in Washington, so were the Georgia events that followed his narrow 1990 victory. After the 1990 census, the Georgia General Assembly worked to redraw the state's political boundaries. By then, Gingrich was one of but two Republican congressmen in the state. The betting at the state capitol was that his longtime foe, Georgia House Speaker Thomas B. Murphy, would use redistricting to wound Gingrich, if not defeat him. In another era, that might have been possible, but the Democratic Party's insistence during

Reagan's first term on renewing and changing the Voting Rights Act of 1965 made the job more difficult. The law, applied primarily in the South, subjects state legislative redistricting decisions to U.S. Justice Department approval.

The act's renewal saw a critical change, one that has been pushing Southern politics toward electoral quotas, or proportional representation of African-Americans. No longer was the test whether politicians "intended" to discriminate against minorities. All that was needed to trigger the Voting Rights Act was to demonstrate the "effects" of discrimination. State legislatures were pressured to "maximize" black voting strength. (The results of the 1990 reapportionments—with their bizarre, serpentine districts scooping up pockets of black voters—were awaiting U.S. Supreme Court review in 1995.) In Georgia, where African-Americans make up 30 percent of the population, the Justice Department insisted that at least three of its 11 congressional districts should be represented by African-Americans.

The law had its intended effect in Georgia with the election in 1992 of three African-American representatives. The election of three additional Republicans, however, surely was not what voting rights activists had in mind. The Democrats had been pressured into a misfire. Because of demographic patterns and the mandates of the Justice Department, Speaker Murphy, despite his best efforts, was unable to redraw Newt's district boundaries to exclude Republicans and include more traditionally Democratic voters. Instead, Murphy threw in the towel. He agreed to move the Sixth District to the most stoutly Republican turf in Georgia—the prosperous northern arc around Atlanta. (Surprisingly, Gingrich's former district, redrawn to help Democrats, elected another Republican, Mac Collins. Dave Worley, too liberal now for a district with fewer black voters, failed to survive a Democratic primary.)

On paper, the new Sixth District was the perfect place for a conservative politician with the vision to pursue national ambitions. The district is among the best educated and most affluent in the South and is home to many of the new "mega churches," with large congregations and allegiances to the

As an eager young professor at West Georgia College, Newt led students on ecological field trips and exposed them to uncoventional theories on space and the future.

Newt took his first campaign plunge in 1974, signing up to run for the Sixth District congressional seat as GOP Chairman Bob Shaw looked on.

(Right) The history professor stepped outside the classroom to campaign hard before Georgia voters, but his first two races for Congress would end in defeat.

(Below) "To persist until you get lucky," is a Gingrich motto. In 1978, after two close losses, he defeated Virginia Shapard and headed for Washington. He shared his election-night happiness with his former wife Jackie (right) and daughters Jackie Sue (second from left) and Kathy (second from right).

As a conservative firebrand, Newt earned media attention and GOP allies for his attacks on the Democratic leadership. Despite a controversy surrounding his book, *Window of Opportunity*, Newt was elected Republican Whip by his colleagues in 1989.

As a boy, Newt dreamed of becoming a zookeeper, and his interest in animal species continues today. He held a 1988 press conference to call for an international ban on ivory.

As Minority Whip, Newt took an increasingly dominant policy role in Washington. He held a 1990 press conference with Sen. Phil Gramm to discuss Middle Eastern issues.

Newt's wife Marianne (right) is also his closest confidant and advisor. She joined Newt's daughter Jackie Sue (center) as 1988 election returns came in.

In a town of workaholics, Newt outpaces all but a few. Here he signs mail while consulting with other GOP congressmen.

"You're killing us," is what President George Bush said to Gingrich in 1990 when the congressman broke with the president over his budget. Gingrich's decision to oppose the tax increases in the agreement with House and Senate Democrats was the defining moment of his career. Still, in 1992, the president and the rebel campaigned together in Atlanta.

Aides have to hustle to keep up with the fast-moving Gingrich. Press secretary Sheila Ward (left) and intern Angela Johnson (center) follow him through a Capitol hallway in 1991.

Newt took the biggest gamble of his career when he attacked Speaker Jim Wright in 1989.

As Whip, Gingrich came under fire for his use of a chaffeured car. In a speech to Georgia Republicans, he defended his actions, but the issue nearly cost him the '92 primary election.

Nearly two decades after trading in his academic career for politics, Newt is still drawn to the classroom. Here he signs autographs for 5th graders at a suburban Atlanta elementary school.

Newt's Renewing American Civilization college course drew rave reviews from students, but was attacked by Democrats and the press for its funding and alleged partisanship. The 10 two-hour lectures offered prescriptions to reform and rebuild American business and political life.

November 9, 1994, Newt and his supporters celebrated a rousing victory over Ben Jones and cheered the news that Republicans would retake the House after 40 years of Democratic control. Newt's lifelong dream of leading the House as Speaker would soon be reality.

Christian Coalition. It is the embodiment of the New South, with few of the rural voters who still blame the Great Depression on Herbert Hoover and the Republicans.

Twenty years ago, the notion of a New South embraced liberal and moderate Democrats who led their party away from the race-based conservatism of a century's practice. They seemed progressive to the national press, while presiding over courthouse business as usual at home. Jimmy Carter was a prime example. Today's New South is different, and the Gingrich Republicans are its political standard-bearers. Some are transplants from the North who bring Republican politics with them. Most are former Democrats from the South's small towns who went away to college and then moved to the metropolitan hubs for opportunity. They are more apt to be white-collar than not, more likely to have chosen to vote Republican than to have inherited a party loyalty. Many are onetime Democrats for whom the party moved too far to the left. The Christian Coalition has mined those voters effectively for more than a decade.

These new Republicans live in pleasant suburban neighborhoods linked by the sprawl and clutter of fast-food chains, convenience stores, and strip shopping centers. They are accused of white flight but in fact, more often they migrated to the suburbs from smaller towns than from troubled cities. They chose their neighborhoods for their schools, their churches, and their interstate-highway access. Thirty years ago, the image of the South was an old sheriff with sunlight reflecting menacingly from his sunglasses. Today that sun glints from 20 and 30 floors of glass office towers from Charlotte to Dallas.

THE BANK THAT SQUEALED ▪ The new Sixth District should have have been a perfect fit for Gingrich, but the congressman initially misjudged the voters. He was confident and comfortable in the more Republican surroundings. Veteran suburban Republican officeholders were able to help him at every turn. He had beaten State Speaker Murphy into surrender. The Republican Whip seemed free of local worries and able to exercise his plan for a Republican majority.

Since the tactics for that plan had called for painting a potrait of a corrupt, arrogant Democratic majority, 1992's unfolding House Bank scandal seemed made to order. It was a three-alarm fire turned into a conflagration by the laggard response of the House leader, Speaker Tom Foley, and the acquiescence of Minority Leader Robert Michel.

The House Bank wasn't really a bank. It was an antiquated payroll service run for the convenience of 435 privileged customers. A 1991 audit revealed thousands of overdrafts over a period of several years. It looked to the public as if one of the perks of Congress was living on an interest-free float. Gingrich went into action, pressing for full disclosure. He demanded names, frequency, and amounts of the overdrafts. Talk shows and editorial pages weighed in with sledge-hammers. What better image to capture the cynicism of the age than that of congressional fat cats who couldn't balance the federal budget, failing even to balance their own.

In April of 1992, an election year, the House Ethics Committee released a mountain of paper. More than 300 former and current members had overdrawn their accounts, usually just before a paycheck was to be posted. The entire lot came to be known as bounced checks.

All across the nation, congressmen were visiting editorial boards and broadcast outlets, humbly trying to explain that the bank wasn't a bank, that payroll deposit postings and statements were tardy and error-filled. Most said they didn't know of overdrafts until the audit and the Ethics Committee investigation. A few congressmen had to explain how their overdrafts just happened to coincide with the weeks right before an election, when campaign cash was short.

Gingrich had check problems of his own. Early on, he had admitted to three checks that might have been rubber, but the official report showed him with 22. The most damaging was one for $9,463—payable to Uncle Sam. Newt had paid his 1989 federal income taxes with a bounced check, a practice that would bring revenuers down the throat of the average Joe

Sixpack who failed to reconcile his bank statement properly. Gingrich argued that he had fought for full disclosure of the scandal, even though it might hurt him.

The firestorm nearly engulfed Congress and surely played a part in the 1994 Republican victory. Previously unconquerable Democrats were swept out in 1992. By 1994, many incumbents were seen as perk-driven, limousine-riding captives of special interests who couldn't balance their own checkbooks.

"E E - Y I - E E - Y I - O O O " ▪ One Georgian who noticed was Jim Lovejoy, a Republican political consultant who operates on populist principle and a rich sense of humor. Lovejoy lives in Cobb County, the population hub of the new Gingrich district. He often has been at odds with the Republican establishment but retains its respect for his deft work unseating entrenched Democrats. He hired on to the campaign of Republican Herman Clark, an earnest state senator perfectly content to be a pillar of his church, a good husband, and an honest legislator.

Clark's challenge to the number-two Republican in the House was seen by most everyone as a fool's errand. He entered the 1992 Republican primary, he said, because he had announced for the seat before the General Assembly moved Gingrich into it. Clark ran a witty, corny version of a political search-and-destroy mission. One radio commercial was sung to the tune of "Old McDonald Had a Farm":

Congressman Newt Gingrich bounced 22 checks,
For more than 26 grand.
With a bounced check here and a pay raise there,
Here a check, there a check, everywhere a bounced check.

The *Atlanta Constitution's* Mike Luckovich penned a cartoon showing Newt looking into a mirror and seeing "the only pompous, perkaholic, check-bouncing, special-interest-driven Washington insider Newt Gingrich hasn't criticized."

In April, Gingrich gave up his government sedan and the $60,000 a year driver/security man that came with his job as

Whip. He was forced to show how he was different from Charles Diggs, Jim Wright, and all the other Capitol Hill insiders he had attacked. Clark didn't make it easy, firing barrage after barrage at Gingrich for overuse of House franking privileges and ties to special interests. Gingrich long has used his frank—official free mailing privileges—more than any other Georgia representative. And for the first time, GOPAC, the fund-raising operation that was the training vehicle for the revolution, also came under fire.

Hostile forces from Washington got in on the act. Ralph Nader's network of "good-government" lobbies formed a political action committee just to work on the Gingrich race. It was an anti-PAC group forming a PAC. Calling itself the Fund for a Clean Congress, it bought television ads calling Gingrich the "Emperor of the Imperial Congress." The Association of Trial Lawyers and several labor unions—historically no friends of Republicans—contributed heavily to Clark simply to defeat Gingrich.

The Gingrich campaign, again run by remote from Washington by Joe Gaylord, had its problems. GOP officeholders in the new district had to beg and cajole to convince Gaylord that trouble lay ahead and that television advertising was vital.

On election night, the crowd that had gathered at the hotel chosen for Gingrich's victory party was shocked. The early returns from Cobb County, which Clark represented in the state senate, were disastrous. As the returns came in from counties where Clark wasn't as well known, Gingrich inched ahead, but not until the early hours of the morning. The final tally was razor-thin. A little-known Republican state senator had gotten 34,702 votes to 35,682 for Gingrich—a margin of fewer than 1,000 votes. The congressman had spent $1 million in the primary against Clark's $160,000.

Gingrich is a cool customer under fire. That night, he joked about his penchant for "landslides" and reflected on what had happened. He was the outsider in the district, even to Republicans. Some voters saw him as a carpetbagger; in Cobb County, Democrats had come out in large numbers to defeat him in Georgia's open primary. Too many voters, he told me, had formed their judgments of him from the Atlanta press, reading for years the attacks in the *Constitution*. A 12-page direct-mail flier had been used to counter that. Its headline was, "There's even more about Newt Gingrich the newspapers haven't told you." The flyer tallied Gingrich's legislative priorities, elements lost in a campaign over congressional perks and pay raises. Exit polling showed that female voters, in particular, seemed uneasy with him for his confrontational, finger-in-the-chest style on television.

T H E D I V O R C E — A G A I N ▪ Those traits would be the focus of the 1992 general election campaign waged by Tony Center, the Democratic nominee. Center was a lawyer unknown to many outside of his family and neighborhood. He wasn't given a chance in such a heavily Republican district, but Georgia Democrats were willing to support him heavily. They knew Gingrich needed a resounding victory to scare off future Democratic challengers in his new district and free him sufficiently from local politics to tend to his national ambitions.

Center's first television ad struck the rawest of nerves. It dragged up the congressman's divorce, asserting that Gingrich had "delivered divorce papers to his wife the day after her cancer operation." It charged that Newt had refused to support his wife and daughters financially, while getting rich on Washington perks. Newt's daughter, Jackie Sue, now Jackie Gingrich Zyla, was angry enough to counter with her own commercial. "My dad has always stood behind and supported me and my sister in everything we have done."

Still, Gingrich had gotten the wakeup call in the primary campaign and was concerned. He decided to attack Center, but not until after he had canvassed friends and worried aloud that he was stooping to his opponent's level. Gingrich, usually the happy campaigner, had no taste for the 1992 race.

"This is the most miserable campaign I've ever been in," he told the *New York Times* that summer. "I've seriously considered just quitting, just saying, 'This filth is so sickening,

I don't want to be part of it anymore.'"

In fact, Newt had moved into his new district with the best of motives. He worked hard to learn the issues that mattered to its various constituencies. He surprised me by remembering that I was a resident of the new turf and asking for thoughts on how to make a difference. Now he was engaged in the most personal of races.

His staff found the perfect vehicle with which to attack Center: his career as a lawyer. The Association of Trial Lawyers of America was spending heavily to defeat Gingrich, so he counterattacked. He aired television and radio commercials spotlighting Center's handling of a divorce case in which a woman had been awarded $500 a month for support for her two children, but didn't pay Center's fee. Center unsuccessfully went to court to try to garnish her support payments. Center called the charge outrageous and inaccurate. At most, he said, only 25 percent of the support payments could have gone to pay legal fees.

As a Gingrich flier noted, "Had he won his case, he would have successfully set a precedent which would have henceforth made child support no longer the property of the children to whom it is awarded, but rather the property of the trial lawyers."

Center, a weak candidate with no experience, managed to win more than 40 percent of the vote. The race proved to Gingrich that even in a Republican stronghold he begins with passionate opponents and high negatives. And female voters remain uneasy about him. The victory margin, while an improvement over his previous "landslides," wasn't quite enough to declare his a permanently safe seat.

HOUNDING NEWT ■ In 1994, Gingrich demolished a Republican primary challenger and then faced Ben Jones, a former congressman who had been redistricted from one seat, lost in 1990 in a race for another, and now was trying a third district. Jones, a former television actor who played Cooter on "The Dukes of Hazzard," has made a career of dogging Gingrich. He picked up the "Boot Newt" banners of past

Gingrich opponents, encouraged by his former Democratic colleagues in Washington.

It was an odd campaign. Jones' views are mostly liberal, and he had little chance. But he used the candidacy to file a series of complaints about Gingrich with the House Ethics Committee. Part of the Democratic effort was to try to pin Gingrich down in Georgia, to prevent him from traveling the nation on behalf of Republican candidates and the Contract With America. After Jones used an ugly epithet about Gingrich in a local alternative newspaper, the congressman had an excuse to refuse to debate him and to continue to travel. Jones tracked Gingrich to Wisconsin and, in a humorous stunt, brought beagles with him to "track" Gingrich in Alabama, all in an effort to show him as a national politico out of touch with the concerns of his Georgia district. The challenger got more coverage outside Georgia than in.

Jones also had some fun. A recovering alcoholic, he has been married several times and has had problems with substance abuse. Of Gingrich's rough personal campaign tactics, Jones said, "Bring him on. I've got more on me than he'll ever have on me." Savvy with the press, Jones used his skill to plant several stories late in the campaign that he was in a close race with the Speaker-to-be. In fact, he was crushed, winning only 37 percent of the vote. Events since the November election show that Jones was more interested in bringing down Gingrich before the House Ethics Committee than in winning his congressional seat.

ANOTHER RUNG ON THE LADDER ■
While he was establishing himself in his new district in 1992, Gingrich had not lost sight of his vision for the nation. He recalls that in late 1992, he was in Florida to visit his friend and contributor, the businessman Owen Roberts. Roberts was angry over the situation in Somalia, where American Marines were going ashore to help save Somalis from starvation. Gingrich and Roberts knew that any positive results would be temporary, and that the U.S. would not stay to build a nation

modeled after American principles.

In a tone of sarcasm, Gingrich asked Roberts, "Why would we think we could teach this to Somalis, when we no longer teach American civilization to our own students?"

As they talked and as they absorbed the day's news, with its ritual catalogue of homicide, abuse, and neglect, they concocted what has become Renewing American Civilization, college lectures for credit, distributed by satellite to other schools and interested groups; and the Progress & Freedom Foundation to raise money for the venture. The actual course was then written by Gingrich with the help of Dr. Jeffrey Eisenach, now the head of the Progress & Freedom Foundation, and Steve Hanser, one of his closest friends and mentors from his days at West Georgia College.

In Washington, the more conservative Republicans had become the dominant group on the GOP side of the House, and their numbers were growing. Even though the GOP lost the White House to Bill Clinton in 1992, that election saw a net increase of 10 Republican seats in the House. Gingrich began to consolidate the power within. Rep. Dick Armey of Texas was elected to the number-three leadership position over Rep. Jerry Lewis of California, a potential rival to Gingrich.

Friends believe that Gingrich was preparing to challenge Bob Michel for Republican leader in 1994. But the showdown, between the two men whose approaches were so different and who represented such different Republican eras, never came. In October, 1993, Michel announced his retirement. Ed Rollins, a Republican campaign guru, told the *Washington Post,* "He [Gingrich] basically drove him out." The Michel-Gingrich relationship could be likened to that of father and rebellious son. The two men tried to hide their differences and worked to get along. But over time, Michel saw his troops congregating more and more in the Whip's office. In a memorable comment to the *Los Angeles Times* in 1991, he said, "Some days, you think of hiring a food taster."

Gingrich scrambled to lock down the votes necessary to succeed Michel. He was able to proclaim within just a few days that he had the necessary commitments and would be elected leader when the official vote was taken after the 1994 elections. Gingrich set about trying to show that he could lead. He was quoted often about his effort to change from rebellious back-bencher to a more mature leader. It is an ongoing battle. As he said to me after becoming Speaker, "I lead with my chin, but I lead."

Michel receded from view as Gingrich rounded up Republican votes to pass the North American Free Trade Agreement, a pact initiated by Bush and supported by Clinton. On another front, Gingrich immediately joined the opposition to the president's first legislative priority—health care reform. Unbeknownst to most Georgia voters, Gingrich had been working on health care issues for years. He drew on the expertise of Gail Wilensky, the head of the Health Care Financing Administration in the Bush administration. Where some Republicans were overwhelmed by Hillary Rodham Clinton's detailed knowledge of the work of her secret health care task force, Gingrich had been studying the issue longer. He told me in the spring of 1994 about a meeting with the First Lady, a session that any reporter would like to have witnessed.

"We had a good discussion," said the Speaker-to-be. "I begged her not to go for the whole reform package that puts at risk one-seventh of the American economy. My advice was to go for four small reforms to see what worked. Try ensuring portability of health insurance when people change jobs. See that preexisting conditions are covered. Take care of malpractice and tort reform. Create medical savings accounts. That sort of thing. If she tries to do it all, she will fail."

And fail she did, in dramatic fashion a few months later, just before the historic elections to come.

THE MACHINE GATHERS SPEED ▪
Gingrich's legislative efforts were conducted in public view, but only reporters who covered him closely saw the fruit of his strategic and tactical models of "vision, strategy, tactics, and projects." With its growing national base of contributors outside the Republican Party apparatus, GOPAC was becoming a machine.

It was apparent at the 1992 Republican Convention in Houston, where Newt's attention was claimed by the national press and the well-heeled, committed GOPAC contributors who rolled to the Astrodome in comfortable buses. Newt was their rock star, while George Bush was merely their candidate—one to be tolerated, a Republican to stave off the Democrats and hold the White House until the movement conservatives came of age.

GOPAC had been founded in 1979 by Pierre S. "Pete" DuPont IV, the governor of Delaware. Its aim was to help develop Republican candidates who could move up the ladder. When DuPont ran for president in 1988, he turned GOPAC over to Gingrich, whose earlier political action committee, the American Opportunity PAC, had done little and raised less.

GOPAC now can be considered the academy of modern Republicanism, the training vehicle for the principles developed by Gingrich through the Conservative Opportunity Society. Since 1991 alone, it has spent $8 million in its work. It might be more accurate to call the committee "Hooked on Politics," for GOPAC has audiotapes for every occasion— more than 9,600 of them by 1995—available to candidates at every level of public life. The audiotape concept was devised by Gingrich and the current governor of Michigan, John Engler. In the new Congress are scores of Republicans who relied on the tapes for ideas, practical advice, or just plain moral support on the lonely drive to yet another rubber-chicken dinner.

In 1994, GOPAC was well enough established to provide a vehicle for a national campaign by a relatively obscure congressman from Georgia who was yet the official leader of the minority party in the House. The Contract With America would nationalize the issues in the campaign without so much as a presidential candidate in the field.

Gingrich visited 127 congressional districts in search of the 40 victories he would need to give the GOP control of the House for the first time in 40 years. He proved to be a superb fund-raiser, by his account raising $3 million in the 1994 campaign. To use his words, he was allowing candidates "to invest their fears in his courage."

Rep. John Linder of Georgia, a longtime friend and associate, calls it "the single most prodigious political output I've ever seen." Linder recalls meeting Gingrich in 1975 and hearing him speak to Georgia groups. "I said to myself," said Linder, "if this guy could bottle this stuff and sell it, he'll be a star."

With the help of GOPAC for selling and the Contract for packaging, he sold it.

SIGN ON THE DOTTED LINE ▪ The written Contract began in 1994 in Room H-219 of the Capitol, the offices of the Whip. Gingrich and his advisers drew up an issues questionnaire for every GOP congressional candidate. Their views were filtered through research focus groups and pollsters such as the new GOP star, Frank Luntz. The results showed them what language worked best to showcase an idea, frame an argument, and hit the voters' hot buttons. But no matter the language used, the Contract With America was a distillation of the ideas Professor Gingrich had been shaping for 20 years, ideas that would transform a failed welfare state.

The Contract served two purposes. It unified candidates and therefore amplified their message. It also would serve as a handy "to-do" list if the Republicans miraculously won control of the House. Arriving in power for the first time in 40 years could easily have led to infighting over priorities and the confusion of "who's on first?" The social issues so important to religious conservatives, for instance, might have dominated bread-and-butter isses. They purposely were omitted. Instead, when the shock of victory wore off, the marching orders were plain. And in carrying them out, the Republicans would be safe: As Gingrich points out, no single item in the Contract failed to attract less than 60 percent polling support.

In H-219, Gingrich planned and organized as if victory were assured. The Whip and soon-to-be Majority Leader, Rep. Dick Armey of Texas, was in charge of organizing 10 task forces. No detail was too trivial for staff study, from office assignments to telephone service. As far as anyone knows, such pre-election planning never had been done in the history of the House. At the time, an outsider might have considered it the sort of foolishness engaged in by perennial candidates— the acts of a Harold Stassen or a Jerry Brown still searching for victory.

Pundits didn't believe it possible. Most projections saw Republicans winning control of the U.S. Senate but falling just short in the House. A search of informed speculation shows the presumed experts looking for gains of 25 to 35 Republican seats. With the cooperation of moderate and conservative Democrats, such a gain would have given Republicans ideological control of the House, but it would not have made Newt Gingrich its Speaker.

Foolishly, the Clinton administration made an issue of the Contract With America, calling it the return of Reaganomics. "Voodoo Two," quipped David Wilhelm, chairman of the Democratic National Committee. Their attacks brought the Contract front and center and nationalized 435 individual House races. With Clinton's popularity down, voters could choose a Republican representative as their vote against the president. Linder put it another way: "They offered security, and we offered freedom. Security is very seductive, but freedom won."

The Contract was signed in September, 1994, in an elaborate event for the cameras in front of the Capitol. Incumbents and candidates, 367 strong, stepped forward in groups to sign it, pens poised in front of red, white, and blue bunting and the Capitol steps above them.

The Contract symbolized accountability: It invited voters to throw the bums out if they hadn't kept their promise to vote on all 10 pieces of legislation in their first 100 days in office. The daring departure from the usual arcane procedural practices of Congress struck a chord. That politicians would swear to carry out a simple, specific agenda for change and vow to be judged by its success was a dramatic departure from business as usual. And Gingrich used apocalyptic language familiar to those who had been listening to him for years.

"Today on these steps we offer this Contract as a first step toward renewing American civilization. If America fails, our children will live on a dark and bloody planet."

Over the next two months, after the Contract had been placed in *TV Guide*, Gingrich carried his laminated copy everywhere, whipping it out of his breast pocket like a rapier to fend off liberal assaults. And on election night, 52 additional seats were claimed for the GOP. Newt Gingrich was to finally achieve his lifelong goal—to be Speaker. In the House were 73 new Republicans, most of them elected with help from GOPAC and the Contract, all of them owing allegiance to Gingrich. Over in the Senate, one-third of the Republican majority of 53 are former members of the Conservative Opportunity Society.

Newt Gingrich had survived two disheartening election defeats in the 1970s. He had hung onto his congressional seat twice by fewer than 1,000 votes. He had contested the senior leadership of his party and rebuked a popular Republican president. Yet here he was, the King of the Hill in one national magazine, the Man With a Vision in another. He was the leader of a new American revolution.

THE CRITICS

"This city is going to be a mean, tough, hard city, and everybody better understand that coming down the road. What you've got in this city is a simple principle. I am a genuine revolutionary; they are the genuine reactionaries. We are going to change their world; they will do anything to stop us. They will use any tool— there is no grotesquerie, no distortion, no dishonesty too great for them to come after us."

CHAPTER 8

GOOD NEWT, BAD NEWT

"I think there are four challenges to the news media that this particular event happens to fit perfectly.

First of all, we really are different. I mean any of you who have boxes you are used to and you are trying to figure out where do we put Speaker Gingrich, just forget it; erase the board. I mean just literally dump everything out of your PC and go back and start over because if you try to cover us by fitting us into any historical pattern of the last 60 years you are just not going to get it.

Second, what we are doing is complex; it is not simple. And every time you try to figure out how to reduce it to a nine-second sound bite, or the one-paragraph explanation, you are going to begin—it's going to take a long time to find the right language because the relationship between hope and opportunity and a work effort and family background—every one of these folks will tell you—there were days they wanted to quit. There were days it wasn't working right. And if you want to understand what Charles Murray tried to get out in his book about welfare it is that when you build a system that makes it easy to quit when you feel bad, you build a system that teaches people to be quitters. And every person here who has succeeded will tell you, and I know this from personal experience having lost twice and campaigned for five years, that it's not easy to rise.

It's particularly not easy to rise if you happen to be born poor. And for two generations we've lied to the poor in America and told them the government will be here soon. You don't have to go out and learn, for example, to show up on Monday. You don't have to learn to stay when you are in a fight with your girlfriend or your boyfriend. You don't have to learn to actually deal with customers when they are unhappy. You can avoid all this; let us send you a check.

The third point I'll tell you is that we represent hope over time, we represent no miracles in a weekend. That over and again you talk to the folks who have done it for real and they'll tell you, it doesn't happen in a day. It doesn't happen in three days. It doesn't fit Secretary Reich's Harvard-based theoretical plan. But it does fit American pragmatism and it does fit the real world.

And fourth, I would suggest to all of you that to make it work you've got to be positive. I think this is going to be the most interesting challenge for the news media. I don't mean by being positive that you all ought to go out and take Dale Carnegie courses. But I mean something very profound—rising from poverty requires that you have hope and that you emphasize the positive rather than the negative half of your experience.

In my case, every time I lost I would come back and say, Okay, now what do I have to learn from that? Many entrepreneurs will tell you they've been bankrupt at least once. And instead of saying well, this is my excuse now to be a victim the rest of my life they said, 'Gee, what did I do wrong? What do I need to learn? How do I do it differently?'

I think it is going to be interesting to see if we can get, for example, the weekend talk show hosts to ask how you could do something, rather than try to find the quick, tricky question to prove you can't do something. It's a totally different mindset. It doesn't mean you shouldn't be critical. Again, everyone here will tell you, they had their friends who ask them tough questions or they would go broke. Not that you [the media] don't need to be critical, but you don't need to be negative and cynical and destructive. And that the tone of a society which is genuinely trying to produce things is totally different than the tone of a society where it's more important to fight than it is to get something done.

If we will listen to the restaurant industry, if we will listen to people who are actually out there working and doing it right now, if we'll go and say don't tell me the next theoretical model from five bureaucrats who have never created a job or hired a person, but do as I did last year. Ask 10 people, as I did, who run McDonald's, who are black, half of them owners and half of them managers: Who do you hire? How do you hire them? How do you train them? What do you do? And then start listening.

And I think you'll find as you watch our hearings a radical difference at two levels. Where the people from the old order tended to hold hearings on victims and pain and failure so they could spend long periods of time studying how bad America was, we are going to bring in people who started at exactly the same place, but who are students of how to rise, how to succeed, how to achieve, how to create. And we are going to ask them to tell us what are you doing right that lets you hire 1,000 people and what do you think the government could do so more people could go out and create systems that hire 1,000 people.

You're going to see a focus again and again on what is the solution. Show us some place that is working. Who's done the best job in America of hiring the hard-core unemployed and actually getting them into productive careers, where then years later they're still working?

Who's done the best job in America of taking people with addiction problems and helping them go through withdrawal and helping them actually succeed? And what you see here is the living real proof—not the theoretical model, not the latest press release from some Washington lobbying group that wants to keep its federal funding— the real proof of real human beings in real families and real lifetime achievement, that it is possible in America to

rise. It is possible to improve yourself. It is possible to
help your children get a better education and have an
even better future."

(Newt Gingrich, remarks to reporters, News Conference
with the National Restaurant Association,
Washington, D.C., January 9, 1995)

In his earliest days, Newt Gingrich didn't believe the press was cynical. Experience had not yet taught him to distrust its representatives. In fact, he enjoyed the company of reporters for the opportunity to learn about media habits and power. When he was a young professor and an underdog candidate for Congress, Georgia newpapers and TV stations were good to him. Newt was brash and exciting. Television news, for obvious reasons, likes pictures. A professor and candidate interested in the environment—leading eager, fresh faces into the Okefenokee Swamp—that was a good visual.

On the campaign trail, Newt spoke sharply and concisely, giving reporters and editors what they wanted: spicy quotes or 22-second sound bites. Unlike those of his parents' political generation, Newt, closer to the baby boomers, had no fears or reservations about television; indeed, he embraced it.

The last decade has seen a sweeping change—both in Gingrich's attitudes and in the huge mass we call media.

By late 1994 and into 1995, Newt was going to war against the *Atlanta Journal* and *Constitution*, seeing his daily Speaker's briefings slip into intellectual mud wrestling and declaring a moratorium on appearances on the Sunday network news broadcasts that shape the week's agenda. The *Washington Post* began an irregular series of stories refuting his facts and anecdotes. The series resembled story-length versions of the "truth boxes" so many newspapers run to clarify campaign commercials. Some had factual merit. Too many resembled nit-picking "gotcha" tricks, hair-splitting distinctions without real differences.

The network news broadcasts began covering him

indulgently, as if Newt were some loud-mouthed kid who needed adult interpretation. The news magazines can't quite decide who he is. On one *Newsweek* cover, a smiling Gingrich is the "Right Face." On another, he's the "Gingrich Who Stole Christmas." Another shows him grimacing under the headline, "How 'Normal' is Newt?" *Time* had him snarling on its cover under the words "Mad As Hell," as an "Uncle Scrooge," and as the "guerrilla" who brought down the House. But the contrast between the magazine covers and the stories inside seem to reflect some internal doubts and divisions. The reporting inside was in most cases an honest, if belated, effort to figure out how the unanticipated came to be and where it would lead. The *Washington Post* produced a first-rate, four-part biographical series. The *Atlanta Journal* and *Constitution* decided to step back for a fresh look, offering a series of biographical pieces by reporters with a sense of local history and tradition.

The more highbrow magazines' approach has been mixed, but often has descended into intellectual pin dancing. A story in the *New Republic* called Gingrich's view of history "grist for middle-brow propaganda." The *New Yorker* resorted to silliness, with a piece titled "Let them eat laptops." In an attempt at cuteness called "Marxism: The Sequel," the *New Yorker*'s Hendrik Hertzberg reached far afield to opine that the Tofflers' Third Wave theory "offers an eerie similarity" to Marxism.

DRIVING UP HIS NEGATIVES ▪ Gingrich argues that much of what was called shooting himself in the foot was not so much his work as that of a hostile press. A study of the national press by the nonpartisan Center for Media and Public Affairs in Washington showed Gingrich receiving 67 percent negative coverage in December, 1994. Stories about Gingrich's positions on welfare were 85 percent negative, and his ethics were criticized by 79 percent of the sources used. President Clinton, said by his spin doctors to be the most mistreated president since Nixon, received 58 percent negative coverage.

The drumbeat of negatives and the portrayals of the Speaker as angry and confrontational hurt him in the opinion polls. Newt has never been, to put it mildly, a resoundingly popular politician. His campaign opponents begin their work knowing that 35 to 40 percent of the electorate won't vote for him under any circumstances. His style inspires strong feelings on both sides. Deep allegiance or intense dislike is common. A *Wall Street Journal*/NBC News Poll in March, 1995, found that 41 percent of those surveyed had a negative impression of him, up from 31 percent negative in January. By a 43-percent to 37-percent margin, more respondents disapproved of his performance as Speaker.

Comfortable as a lightning rod, Newt has never worried much about polls. He is fond of remembering Daniel Yankelovich's distinction between public opinion and public judgment: The former is what people think at any given moment. The latter is what results after weeks or months of national debate on an issue. Gingrich, the historian, prefers to win the longer-term judgments.

The Speaker's own view of his press relations suggests he doesn't plan to soften his image. "Nothing which has ever been said about me," he said early in 1995, "is comparable to what was said about Lincoln or what Jefferson and Hamilton said about each other through papers that they subsidized. This is a rough business. This isn't Russia. This isn't China. This isn't a controlled press. This country is the most rough-and-tumble, brutal political system in the world. Except that we don't kill each other."

He has thick skin, indeed, to remain philosophical after Clinton political consultant Paul Begala called him "a draft-dodging, pot-smoking, deadbeat dad who led a pro-obscenity campaign in college."

Gingrich fans might think his high negative ratings in polls are the product of press distortions of such issues as proposals for orphanages for abandoned and mistreated children, or his vow to eliminate federal funds for the Corporation for Public Broadcasting. And the hammering of Democratic ethics charges has chipped away at his approval rating. But the

Speaker himself has done a good deal to roil the waters. When he tells a group of business leaders that many newspaper editorial boards contain socialists, for example, he can expect grenades thrown back his way. And when he suggests that business executives consider withholding advertising from newspapers opposed to their views, he is hitting journalists where they live.

Of the editorial board comments, The *Post*'s Richard Cohen wrote that it was "a statement so preposterous, I can only assume he meant 'socialites.'" He went no further. But isn't it possible—even likely—that the *Post*'s editorial board includes a person who endorses a guaranteed annual income or similar share-the-wealth schemes? And isn't it likely that a member or two of a major editorial board believes in nationalizing some industries?

To call someone a socialist is not necessarily to question that person's patriotism. In the press reaction to the socialist tag was the suggestion that somehow Gingrich was reviving McCarthyism. It is a case of the offended protesting too much. Socialism has a lengthy American tradition, even if it is now on the wane. After all, President Clinton's Secretary of Labor, Robert Reich, proudly called himself a democratic socialist in the days after his Rhodes scholarship. As Gingrich said, "I'd be glad to get you a collection of editorials that only make sense if people believe that government's good and the free market is bad."

RETURN TO BOYS TOWN ▪ Yankelovich's "public judgment" will be some time in coming. For now, Gingrich, a man of two-hour college lectures, is dealing with the realities of journalistic shorthand and absence of context from reporters. It is not a new problem for public officials, but it is intensified when a counterrevolutionary set of ideas is laid before the public. Many in the mainstream press had not been exposed to discussions in conservative circles that are old hat to people such as Gingrich. His remarks on orphanages, for example, were drawn from years of discussion on how best to solve the problem of children who lack supervision and structure. Gingrich's comments spawned a score of magazine covers, revived interest in the work of Charles Dickens, inspired the public to greater generosity for Father Flanagan's Boys Town operations, and unleashed hundreds of letters to the editor about how orphanages had saved young lives. The press reacted with surprise to Newt's suggestion of finding stable homes for troubled children, yet such suggestions have been a staple of conservative discussion for years. Two years before Newt's orphanage remarks, the former Labor Secretary, Lynn Martin, wrote a *New York Times* op-ed piece advocating group homes for pregnant teenagers in unstable situations and for children of the addicted and pathological. Even Clinton's Secretary of Health and Human Services, Donna Shalala, admitted under persistent questioning by the House Ways and Means Committee that group homes are used widely today. But neither of the officials was accused of wanting to rip children from the arms of their parents and pack them off to modern-day workhouses.

The press expressed more shock at Gingrich's blunt characterizations of his political opponents. When Newt told a network audience that the Clinton administration was characterized by "counterculture McGoverniks," the McCarthyism warning klaxon sounded in the press's ear yet again. (Gingrich maintains he said "McGovernites.") What the mainstream press did *not* do was acknowledge the accuracy of the description. Those in what Gingrich calls the "elite press" failed to mention that Bill Clinton ran George McGovern's campaign in Texas in 1972, ably assisted by one Hillary Rodham. The extent of the Clintons' commitment to McGovern and the counterculture is documented painstakingly in *First in His Class*, the 1995 Clinton biography by the *Washington Post*'s David Maraniss. Likewise the press seems not to understand that Gingrich uses the year 1965 as his great cultural divide—the year that good intentions gave way to the erosion of shared values and the construction of the modern welfare state.

The media reacted similarly when Gingrich quoted a law enforcement source as saying "as many as 25 percent of the

White House staff had used drugs in the last four or five years." It was, to be sure, a dangerous comment without supporting documentation. But a House Republican, Frank Wolf of Virginia, had raised the same question in the past, noting the postponement of drug tests for White House staffers when Clinton took office and the issuance of a large number of temporary passes that circumvented drug-testing rules.

The press reaction to Gingrich's views perhaps is understandable. During four decades of Democratic domination of Congress, the national press learned to be discerning about the Democratic agenda and its regional and philosophical shadings, while adding only the occasional paragraph or two describing the Republican view. Rare was the reporter such as David Broder, who saw Republican trends and movements building steam. After November 8, 1994, much of the national press was hearing Gingrich's views for the first time. They knew him only as an ethical bomb thrower, or a rebel who turned on President Bush, or a loony futurist. No wonder their labels, with their implications of fascism and cultural nihilism, are so harsh. As my father used to say, "I can't understand him. We went to different schools together."

CONFRONTING CYNICISM ▪ Gingrich is a thorough student of the press and its history. He considers the national press part of the intellectual elite. To him, the press bias is cultural, not partisan. Yet because those he calls the cultural elite tend to vote Democratic, it has the same effect. He traces today's journalistic cynicism to H. L. Mencken, an intellectually acceptable bomb thrower of his day.

"Mencken came to life from a standpoint of extraordinary cynicism," said Gingrich in his lectures, "and he became for the journalism schools and for much of the modern media the sort of archetype of the good critical cynic who stands aloof from the game and who is all-wise and all-knowing and all-contemptuous. Now, the problem with that is that cynicism combined with moralism to produce antipolitics. So now you have these morally superior people who are inherently cynical who dislike the process of politics."

The "all-wise and all-contemptuous" school of journalism can be seen in the "gotchas" of Washington coverage. Some are amusing. Most aren't.

Shortly after becoming Speaker, Gingrich told his college class that women were not suitable for combat because after 30 days in a ditch they are susceptible to infections. It became the firestorm of the week. His parallel comment that men were born to hunt giraffes was turned into high comedy. But students in his class knew he was exaggerating about male and female traits to make a larger point: Women have skills that make them better suited for many military specialties other than combat. Amid the coverage of the comments, it was next to impossible to find a news story on the effects of extended field duty on female combatants. And it was impossible not to hear Rep. Pat Schroeder lampooning him by suggesting that no men she knew had a desire to hunt giraffes.

"Occasionally you get taken grotesquely out of context," he said later, "but that's fine. It is part of the process of getting the message out and frankly, even the things that were the least in context did send a signal to a lot of people: 'Oh, there's a course.'"

"All-wise" reporters passed on exploring whether women on the front lines were more susceptible to infection than men, yet they have been quick to counter attacks on liberals. The clearest example was the treatment of Gingrich's statement that he could not understand the defense of the welfare state by "liberal Democrats, standing in front of the monstrosity they have created, their public housing projects for the poor, their public schools that are illiteracy traps for the poor." A day later, he said, "There are public housing projects where there are lots of people who don't ever see anybody who goes to work."

The *Washington Post* leaped into action, accusing him of blaming "liberal Democrats for creating public schools, public housing projects and all of their well-known problems." The *Post* intoned that the nation's oldest public school, Boston Latin, "was established in 1635—long before either of today's major political parties was formed." The story went on to contradict Gingrich on housing, saying that most massive high-rise projects were built in the 1950s, but did not point out that the explosion in new projects came in the '60s as a result of the Great Society.

Newsrooms and editorial boards have a long history of conflict with each other. So perhaps it was no suprise that the *Post*'s newsroom wasn't in sync with the paper's editorial-page editor, Meg Greenfield.

"Gingrich is quick-bright," Greenfield wrote for *Newsweek* in 1994. "He is a strategist, and he is tireless—the one who is still standing there fighting and/or nagging and/or driving everyone crazy after all the others have had enough and want to call it a day. He escapes the pigeonholes people are always trying to put him in, because his views on issues, while overall very conservative, are in some respects radical and unexpected and politically shrewd."

Using Television ▪ The Speaker has inspired similar reactions in journalists for years. I remember a time when neither Gingrich nor I suspected the other of cynicism.

One day in October, 1976, Gingrich walked into my office at WXIA-TV in Atlanta. I was new to the station and the state and wondering mainly how to cover Jimmy Carter if he won the presidency. Unlike most television news directors, surrounded by the fires and accidents and shootings that are the staples of broadcast news, I was a political junkie. It was politics and policy that always had texture and passion for me, ever since leaving newspapers in the late 1960s to cover Gov. Nelson Rockefeller and Erastus Corning, the legendary machine mayor of Albany, New York, for the CBS affiliate there.

I knew nothing about Gingrich. He was running against an incumbent and he was a college professor with a cadre of young admirers. In truth, I was flattered he wanted to talk with the boss when he might have been better off cultivating reporters on the staff. (It wasn't until 17 years later that I learned his visit might have been calculated. The candidate training tapes for GOPAC, Newt's political action committee, make special mention of the need to visit local television news directors. "They are the central nervous system" of coverage, say Newt and his chief political theorist, Joe Gaylord.)

That first meeting in 1976 paid off for the station in many ways. In 1978, when Gingrich finally won election, WXIA-TV got him live on the air before our competitors. He remembered we'd shown some interest. But more important, those were the first of almost 20 years of conversations about the strengths and shortcomings of the press. Newt loves to talk, and every journalist likes to navel-gaze about the news business.

It's amusing to see some of the cries of outrage from the national press over Gingrich's many recent lectures on press behavior. He loves the battle, and he needs the press the way some men need women: Can't live with 'em; can't live without 'em. What most don't see is his faith that journalists seek fairness. One of his earliest mentors was the Pennsylvania editor, Paul Walker. He holds David Broder of the *Washington Post* in high regard and loves to banter with the Sam Donaldsons of the electronic world. In a Broder, he sees a penetrating analyst. In a Donaldson, he sees his own combative, blustery traits.

WAR WITH THE HOMETOWN PAPER ▪ Early in his career, Gingrich was a favorite of the *Atlanta Constitution*. He respected the veteran political columnists there and won the endorsement of the editorial page, chiefly because he broke with the Old South on racial matters. Bill Shipp, the dean of Georgia political writers, was associate editor of the *Constitution* editorial pages in those days. "We were looking for a liberal to get behind," he said, "and we thought Gingrich was progressive on race and the environment."

The *Constitution* also cited his "freshness and imagination." But the paper broke with him over the harsh tone of his winning 1978 campaign against state Sen. Virginia Shapard, a figure well liked by those who covered the Georgia General Assembly.

In the 1980s, the morning *Constitution* and its older sibling, the afternoon *Atlanta Journal*, drew further apart editorially. The *Constitution* moved left and the *Journal* moved right. Their views on Gingrich could give readers whiplash. The *Constitution*'s editorial-page editor through those years, Tom Teepen, portrayed Gingrich as "loopy," "dangerous," and, that favorite of the left, "mean-spirited." He suggested that even when Gingrich chose a position akin to the newspaper's, it was only because of partisan self-interest.

In 1985, Shipp had abandoned hope for the man he once endorsed. "The gadfly of Congress and the star of C-Span TV has become something of a laughingstock on the national scene," he wrote. "By implication that makes those who sent him to Washington laughable too." (Gingrich got the last laugh on that. His Sixth District of Georgia includes the Shipp household.)

The Atlanta newspapers, both owned by the family of the late Ohio Gov. James M. Cox, the Democratic presidential nominee in 1920, tend to pursue a liberal agenda through their combined news staffs. Save for the conservative outpost on the *Journal*'s editorial page, the papers have had trouble coming to grips with the shrinking city center and the widening Republican ring of affluent suburbs around their city. Circulation has been stagnant and has not kept pace with the growth of metro Atlanta.

If there is a relationship, the Atlanta newspapers haven't seen it. In 1994, the *Constitution* endorsed 10 Democrats for Congress in the state's 11 congressional districts. The one Republican it endorsed, Jack Kingston of Savannah, was running against an unemployed laborer.

The paper's failure to endorse Gingrich was not startling in the context of years of attacks that picked up steam in late 1986. That year, the respected editor of the papers, Jim Minter, was bumped upstairs to a corporate position in an effort to elevate the quality of the *Journal-Constitution* management. Minter knew Georgia and its sensibilities. He knew that descendants of brave yeoman farmers could be pushed only so fast into change; as a result, he had sought a rough balance between the two newspapers.

He was replaced as editor by Bill Kovach, the Washington bureau chief of the *New York Times*, who promised that the *Journal* and *Constitution* would become "world-class newspapers." Kovach lived and breathed the political wars and infused them with lively coverage, often at the expense of local news. He hired and trained a staff of young loyalists, mostly from outside the South. They were the kinds of reporters who counted scalps more than they reflected the community they served.

Kovach was a Democrat by tradition, as a wise Cox editor would be. While he generally was fair, some of his subordinates had different ideas. After one election, the newspaper had carried a picture of a winning Republican congressman on the front page.

"That's the last ___ing time we'll ever have a shot of a ___ing Republican on the front of this newspaper!" shouted the assistant managing editor for local news to an embarrassed newsroom.

Newt Gingrich, however, was undaunted by any unfavorable coverage. In 1987, we met at a restaurant south of Atlanta for an interview. As usual, the state of the Fourth Estate came up.

"You ought to be happy as can be with this new crowd from Washington," he told me. I disagreed.

"For these guys," I said, "columns aren't labeled as such. News stories are the opinion pieces. And they hate you."

"But they know their politics," said the congressman. "They care about it, and they can be converted." He went on to describe several meetings and bull sessions with Atlanta newspaper management that he took to mean a new openness.

Months later, over a beer after a session of the 1988 Republican Convention, I reminded Gingrich of several recent hits on him that he believed were unfair.

"Fool me once," he said ruefully.

But he has been fooled twice and more. He likes reporters and editors. He enjoys the daily Speaker's press conference— now televised on C-Span for the first time ever. His friend and biographer, Mel Steely, is aware of Gingrich's sunny faith in the press.

"We've been telling him for years that they won't change," said Steely. "We've urged him to fight back and cut off the hostile and unfair ones, but he won't. He always believes he can get them to come around to his point of view."

A FINAL STRAW ▪ Problems between Gingrich and the Atlanta newspapers escalated in 1993, when he began planning and teaching his Renewing American Civilization course. Aggressive reporters began to explore the links between the course and GOPAC, his campaign recruitment and training vehicle and part of what has become known as "Newt Inc."

The stories suggested a political motive for the course and claimed it would be partisan in nature. Later stories noted the link between contributors and firms and individuals who were highlighted in the lectures. The newspapers campaigned to have GOPAC's contributor lists made public. The editorial pages agreed (this writer included).

As the sparring went on, a certain amount of one-upmanship came to amuse political junkies. When the *Constitution* failed to endorse Gingrich, his response was to augment the *Journal*'s endorsement by buying a full-page ad in both Atlanta newspapers that reprinted his endorsement by the *Marietta Daily Journal*, a suburban paper with long family ties to Georgia's conservative Democrats.

What finally ended the Speaker's indulgent attitude toward the Atlanta newspapers came the day before the '94 election. The *Constitution*'s editorial page featured a recap of its endorsements, covering most of the editorial page. On the op-ed page ran the regular cartoon of Mike Luckovich, a talented and funny young artist and commentator who was awarded the Pulitzer Prize in 1995 for editorial cartooning.

That day he drew a hospital room. In bed was an elderly woman representing the voters in Gingrich's district. In the cartoon, Newt was flanked by two young women drawn as cleavage-displaying bimbos representing special interests. The caption had Gingrich asking for a divorce.

The visual reference to the allegation that Gingrich had asked his first wife for a divorce while she was recovering from cancer surgery sent Gingrich into a cold rage. He was infuriated that his daughters, who were with him on the visit that his foes have exploited, were portrayed as, well, women of the night.

Newt unsuccessfully demanded an apology. Then he declared war. He refused at first to speak to anyone from the *Journal* or *Constitution* and talked of barring their reporters from his press events. He went so far as to have newspaper personnel removed from his gala election-night celebration (including this writer).

Since then, a rough compromise of sorts has been reached. When *Journal* and *Constitution* reporters ask him questions at press events, he responds. By the end of the first 100 days of the new Congress, he was continuing to refuse any requests for extended interviews, though he did tell me he was relaxing the rules for the newspapers' Washington correspondent, Jeanne Cummings.

The *Journal* editorial page has continued to analyze and generally support Gingrich initiatives, if not all of his off-the-cuff remarks. Meanwhile, the *Constitution* escalated its attacks. In late 1994, an editorial said, "He has always been a man of barely restrained intellectual arrogance, and the recent election seems to have removed the small bit of self-doubt that once leavened his haughtiness. In the bright lights of the television studios, surrounded by adoring colleagues, basking in applause and attention, he seems to have cast aside humility in favor of a full and loving embrace of himself."

The Speaker responds in kind, confident that the marketplace has proven the wisdom, in this instance, of firing back at those who buy ink by the barrel.

"The dilemma of the newsroom and the editorial boards is a different dilemma [from those who hate politics]," he said in 1995. "It is, on the one hand, how do they cover a legitimate skeptic? The difference between a skeptic and a cynic? A skeptic says, I'd like to believe you're sincere, but you've got to convince me. A cynic says, I know you're not sincere.... So now you have a devastatingly more cynical, devastatingly more adversarial system, which makes it harder to report the truth. Because the truth isn't always cynical. The truth is often romantic and wonderful. America is a great country with good people. And you're not allowed to report that because that would clearly not be cynical enough and you'd be laughed at in the newsroom."

COUNTING ON THE "NEW MEDIA" ▪ The *Constitution*'s attacks and its election-eve cartoon raised Gingrich's hackles. But as the media expand to include more alternatives, the opinion of him in the nation's largest newsrooms means a good deal less than it once did.

The Second American Revolution was oppposed by the so-called mainstream media—the national newspapers and networks—but roundly supported by the alternative media. Gingrich knows, for instance, that radio broadcaster Rush Limbaugh was a nuclear-sized megaphone against Clinton and for the more populist House Republicans. (Freshman Republicans call themselves the Ditto-Head Caucus after the name Limbaugh's loyal listeners have given themselves.)

At Gingrich's swearing-in, talk-radio hosts (liberal and conservative) were given broadcast space in the Capitol for the first time. After all, exit polls of voters in 1994 showed that talk-radio listeners were far more likely to vote Republican.

In his humblest moments, Gingrich describes himself as something less than an original thinker. "It's not me," he told me once. "I'm the product of an enormous extended network. I'm the energy and the best collector of the data."

If Gingrich, then, is the synthesizer, Limbaugh is the sound system. And Limbaugh simplifies complicated issues.

Talk radio isn't the only force challenging the big newspapers and networks. To counter liberal distortions, Gingrich "truth squads" also have put down homestead stakes on the computer frontier. Gingrich has put the proceedings of the House of Representatives on-line for computer users and has launched a service called Thomas (for Thomas Jefferson), putting the bills and resolutions of the House in cyberspace, available to anyone on-line with a computer. His lectures are available on the Internet through various on-line services. Gingrich also conducts a weekly discussion program on National Empowerment Television, a cable outlet developed by longtime Gingrich ally Paul Weyrich.

Gingrich can be calculating about the uses of the new media and the place of the old. In the summer of 1994, I argued in a column that the Georgia Board of Regents had erred in ruling to prohibit sitting politicians—such as Newt—from lecturing at state universities. That day, I met with Newt and one of his rising stars, John Kasich of Ohio, now the chairman of the House Budget Committee. Kasich had seen the column in the weekend paper and was quick to praise it. Gingrich, returning to our table from talking to a constituent, took a glance at it, then dismissed its author as if he were an appendage of a pencil press so antiquated as to be irrelevant.

"Yeah, this is great," he said. "It'll play big on the radio talk shows Monday morning. That's what newspaper columns are for these days."

But the mainstream press—the one Gingrich describes as cynical and antipolitics—isn't dead yet. It doesn't care much for "Newt Inc." and isn't likely to back away from investigating his ventures, nor does it care much for Gingrich's belief in a religious America, one bound and determined to put religion back in the public square. When religious issues come before Congress, the mainstream press is likely to take a dim view. It is irreligious, if not anti-religious. No better example can be found than the New York editors Gingrich once welcomed to the Atlanta newspapers. In a region where 78 percent of respondents profess belief in angels, those editors changed the title of the religion page in the Saturday *Journal-Constitution* to "Ethics." It was as if they believed the millions of people who attended churches and synagogues went there not to worship, but to debate the works of Greek philosophers.

CHAPTER 9

FREEDOM OF RELIGION

"I want to raise an issue that is fairly revolutionary and where I'm very, very grateful to Reinhardt College for giving me the academic freedom to actually talk about this, because this is something which probably would get me kicked off of a number of campuses, and that is, I want to suggest to you that faith is central to personal strength.

I'm not here to proselytize either for Christianity or Judaism or anything, but I'm here to talk as a historian about the importance of faith to personal strength. So what I want to suggest to you is that it's amazing the centrality of faith. I'm going to give you, for example, '24 hours a day,' which is Alcoholics Anonymous' program for something to read every day. And they give you something—literally every day you get one page. This is for the first of January, the prayer for the day: 'I pray that God will guide me one day at a time in the new year. I pray that for each day, God will supply the wisdom and the strength that I need.'

Now notice that—every day they have—at the bottom, they have a meditation, they have a prayer, and they have a little thought, and the idea is that if you're a recovering alcoholic—and I got these books because a good friend of mine, we were talking, I was going through a crisis in my life. It wasn't alcohol, but it was just a whole sense of coping with tension and pressure, and he was in Alcoholics Anonymous, and he said to me, 'These are the finest books you'll ever read about being human, and

*their humanness starts with "I am weak. My strength has
to come from a Supreme Being."'*

*Here's what they talk about, the 12 traditions. This
book is still in print, still very widely used around the
world, and it starts with the sense of faith, that only by
giving our problems to a Supreme Being can we find the
strength from the Supreme Being to begin to recover from
alcoholism. [It's] a very, very different model than you
might expect and one which since it wouldn't be taught
on most campuses and could not be discussed in the elite
news media, you couldn't explain as a core step towards
replacing the welfare state in a healthy way.*

*If it turns out that faith is central to an ability to have
personal strength and that faith gives you the ability to
think beyond your immediate selfishness and therefore
helps you leave the culture of poverty and move into a
culture of opportunity based on a longer time horizon,
and if that's an objective fact, then there is a whole
question about how do you reshape public policy.*

*Now, I'm going to say something else which is very
hard to debate on college campuses because of what
Carter described as the culture of disbelief. But let me
assert to you that there's a reason why voluntary school
prayer mattered, and the reason goes from the concept of
being endowed by our Creator and getting authority from
a Supreme Being.*

*I had a very bright student in the class who said, 'Well,
do you really think voluntary school prayer matters that
much?' And I suddenly realized that I really did think it
mattered that much, that I think we are crazy to have
driven it out. As George Gilder said on 'The Progress
Report,' a TV show that we do on NET every Tuesday
night, George Gilder, who is a fairly famous author, said:
We've now replaced opening the day in some schools in
New York with a prayer with opening it by practicing
putting a condom on a banana. He said: Now, you tell
me if you think this was an effective substitute. But as I
began, the student was really adamant. He said: Why*

does it matter? He said: You really think 30 seconds matter? And I suddenly realized the reason it matters is it establishes at the beginning of the day the concept of a hierarchy. That the teacher is an intermediary between the Creator who is endowing us with our unalienable rights and us. Teacher's not just there as a bureaucrat paid by the state to force us to be obedient while they take homeroom, which is what they've become.

But the minute you accept the notion that there is a— what in the Middle Ages was called the great chain of being—the minute you accept the notion that there is a relationship between you and a Supreme Being—I'll keep using the nonreligious word of the Declaration of Independence, because I assume that's legal even on television and talk about the Creator, since that's the word the founding fathers used—if there is a Creator and your rights are endowed by the Creator, then there is a direct bond between you and the Creator.

Now, this is not violation of church and state. They're not teaching you to be a Catholic or to be Jewish or to be Muslim or to be Baptist or Methodist. They're teaching you basic principles of morality and basic principles of relating to personal strength as an act of faith in a Creator.

Now if you're going to say, well, America's not really about that, fine, then you have to repeal the Declaration of Independence. But you've now changed decisively the core psychological component that has made America unique, because part of our fierce independence and pride comes from this notion that since he's endowed by the Creator and she's endowed by the Creator, they have equal right to have their own opinion.

I think—and it took me, I guess, 20 years to figure this out, and it came to me literally trying to explain personal strength—I think that the reason voluntary school prayer matters a lot is that it starts the day by reestablishing the bond and by saying: What we're going to do the rest of the day, we're going to do by people the Creator cares for and by people who are trying to live out the endowment we've been given. And at that moment, you have changed psychologically who the teacher is, and you've changed the entire relationship in the classroom. And so I want to suggest that we have some very fundamental questions to look at."

(Newt Gingrich, from the Renewing American Civilization lectures, Reinhardt College, Waleska, Georgia, 1995)

In viewing and reading all 60 hours of Gingrich's Renewing American Civilization lectures, what jumps out most is how Professor Gingrich weaves belief in a Creator through almost every lecture. Yet reviewing close to 100 interviews and meetings with him in the last 18 years yielded not a single page of notes that mention religion, except for references to his efforts to permit voluntary public school prayer and the parliamentary maneuvering to open school buildings to religious groups.

Atlanta attorney Randy Evans, a very close friend of the Speaker who has known him for 20 years, said Newt's emphasis on faith in his lectures was new to him. "The religious conservatives are among Newt's strongest supporters," Evans said, "but you'll never hear him mention Jesus or talk religion. He just never mentions it." His thought was echoed by Pat Gartland, Georgia director of the Christian Coalition, who works closely with Gingrich. "He doesn't talk about faith much," Gartland said. "But I played football for Bear Bryant, and he didn't say much either, but I knew he was with us." He ascribes the absence of religious conversation to Gingrich's businesslike approach to political tactics and strategy.

Just about every history of Gingrich's career includes the story by his former student and aide, Lee Howell, about when he first began writing speeches for Gingrich and the candidate asked him to remove any Biblical references or phrases such as

"God's will." Howell quotes the young candidate as having doubts about his faith and an aversion to using religion for political purposes. Howell's comments are always presented so as to suggest that Gingrich is a hypocrite.

But Gingrich's avoidance of religion as a campaign device isn't necessarily inconsistent with the Speaker Gingrich of today, who lectures about faith as central to personal accomplishment and cites historical texts on the part that belief in God played in the founding of the Republic.

PUBLIC PROFESSION OF FAITH ▪ In a cynical world, it is tempting to ascribe Gingrich's recent more public emphasis on belief to the Southern and Republican politics of today. In the South, where fundamentalist and evangelical Protestant denominations hold so much sway, politicians don't hesitate to wear their faith on their sleeves. The Southern Baptist Convention, after all, is the largest Protestant denomination in the world. In the South, the modern is often surprised by the traditional. A recent governor of Georgia, for instance, banned alcohol from the governor's mansion. Biblical allusions are the stuff of daily discourse, and churches are primary campaign venues.

But these Southern traditions are not part of Newt's history. He was reared in the Lutheran Church and its mostly conservative wing, the Missouri Synod. He grew up hard by the severe Amish believers of central Pennsylvania. He jokes about worshipping with Army chaplains during his boyhood, "praying in whatever denominations they represented." He recalls being a Methodist acolyte for a time. When he married Jackie and moved to West Georgia College, he was a deacon in the First Baptist Church of Carrollton. After their divorce, he joined the New Hope Baptist Church in Fayetteville, then the largest church in the most Republican county in his district.

Its pastor, Rev. Dwight Reighard, is a leader in the Southern Baptist Convention, a body grown more fundamentalist and conservative with each bruising convention it holds. Reighard holds the congressman in high regard. Still, in 1988, when religious conservatives moved to take over the Georgia delegation to the Republican Convention, Gingrich was conspicuously absent from the infighting. It probably was more smart politics than questionable faith.

Gingrich always has avoided the pitfalls of other Southern politicians who, by their references to "Jesus Christ as personal savior" run the risk of alienating Jews, Muslims, and others.

In avoiding religious rhetoric, Gingrich is heeding the words of Ralph Reed, the executive director of the Christian Coalition and another Ph.D. in history (from Emory University). In his book, *Politically Incorrect*, Reed points out the political pitfalls of using the language of the church in a secular forum:

"....we must persuade people rather than preach. The evangelical idiom with which we are comfortable in propagating the gospel is neither appropriate nor effective in a political context. Those who share our faith may find the quotation of Scripture in support of a particular policy compelling, but it is likely to fall on deaf ears in the larger society."

Gingrich, ever the loquacious public man of a thousand quotes, isn't quick to discuss publicly the details of his most personal beliefs. Beneath some of his personal comments is the hint of a conversion experience. The tortured quotes by Gingrich describing his marital difficulties in 1987 and 1988 point to a man searching for meaning, seeking respite from his driven, 18-hour days.

A man who "cried three or four times a week" often turns to whiskey or worse. Gingrich skipped the whiskey but went straight for the cure. He was led by a friend to the guidebooks of Alcoholics Anonymous and its 12-step program to take control of one's life. As he stresses, that control starts with faith and prayer. He also emphasizes that the AA program depends on individuals helping others, with no publicity or bureaucracy. His personal faith may be something like that.

When I asked him about those years, he seemed surprised that my question dealt with religion and faith. "I went through more pain then [over his differences with Marianne] than I would have thought possible other than cancer," he said. "But it was personal. There are two things people don't get about me. First is that I am an Army brat so I grew up around men for whom 'stand and die' is a reasonable way of life. Second, when I was three years old, I really did see my grandfather die, or he died shortly after I saw him, and that led me to a profound, total commitment to God. I knew then, therefore, I'm never totally alone. You know the quote, 'Here I stand, God rest my soul, I can do no other.'"

A MORAL REAWAKENING ▪ On the role of faith and morality in society, Gingrich has been consistent since first he sought office. When Newt announced for Congress in 1976, it was clear where he stood. "Our deepest need is for leaders who have a commitment to morality above winning. Above all, we need leaders who bring their private sense of right and wrong into the public arena."

When Gingrich searched for positive alternatives to replace the welfare state, he found history underscoring the centrality of belief. He notes, for instance, that John Wesley and Methodism in the last century saved England from a revolution by offering a creed and a work ethic to the laborers displaced by industrialization. Gingrich would like to see a similar "great awakening" for the information age, the Third Wave. In that, interestingly, he is aligned with Hillary Rodham Clinton, who was known in Arkansas for carrying her Methodist creed to the young as part of her "politics of virtue."

Since Gingrich believes in God, not government as godlike supreme arbiter, his call for a society of citizen-activists rings true. The community-based, compassionate relationships necessary to that vision are more likely to come from churches, synagogues, and mosques than from the government. He is quick to point out that the U.S. is the only nation founded on a creed—that all rights come from the Creator.

INVOKING JEFFERSON ▪ To listen to Gingrich's lectures and speeches is to hear a deist in the mold of Thomas

Jefferson, a believer in a Creator but one who is leery of sectarian beliefs. Many of the founding fathers were deists, rationalists who believed that nature demonstrated the existence of God and formal religion was superfluous.

Gingrich is a student of the founding father, James Madison. He knows that Madison also changed his mind on the role of public religion. Madison sought election to the first Congress of 1789 and found himself in a tight race with James Monroe. Madison opposed the Bill of Rights to the Constitution, believing it duplicated state protections. But a visit to Baptists who were being mistreated in the Commonwealth of Virginia convinced him that the First Amendment, then referred to as "the rights of Conscience," was necessary. With Baptist support, he defeated Monroe.

Gingrich uses Jefferson to make his points. In a speech to state legislators in late 1994, he quoted Jefferson's words, inscribed upon the Jefferson Memorial: "I have sworn hostility upon the altar of God Almighty against all forms of tyranny over the mind of man." Gingrich, with more than a trace of sarcasm, turned the tables on those who would have a nation not with freedom *of* religion but with freedom *from* religion:

"Now it does strike me as slightly strange that this man of who all of my liberal friends assure me did not believe in God, decided that it was on God's altar that he would swear eternal hostility [against tyranny]. But I'm sure that was probably just a little PR trick of the period."

In a 1994 speech at the Heritage Foundation, Gingrich recalled an England in which Catholics and Jews couldn't run for office and where the government used the power of taxation to force adherence to the Anglican Church. He noted the religious sentiments of Lincoln, Jefferson, Madison, and, in particular, Benjamin Franklin. Gingrich's voice rose as he recalled a 1787 letter from Franklin to Washington:

"'I have lived, sir, a long time. And the longer I live, the more convincing proofs I see of this truth, that God governs the affairs of men. And if a sparrow cannot fall without His notice, is it probably that an empire can rise without His aid?'"

This, Gingrich noted, was neither Jerry Falwell nor Pat Robertson. He went on to quote an exhortation written by Franklin Roosevelt to read the Bible, distributed along with copies of the Good Book to thousands of troops in World War II. He read his favorite quote from Tocqueville's *Democracy in America*: "Religion in America takes no direct part in the government of society, but it must be regarded as the first of their political institutions."

TOWARD VOLUNTARY SCHOOL PRAYER ▪ Religion has always had a strong but uneasy relationship with conservatives. Robert Nisbet's important book, *Conservatism*, traces the tensions. "In very large degree," he wrote, "the conservative support of religion rested upon the well-founded belief that human beings, once they have got loose from major orthodoxy, are likely to suffer some measure of derangement, or loss of equilibrium." Nisbet believes that "civil" religion—a religion in which transcendent beliefs are reflected in civil and religious traditions such as Thanksgiving and Christmas—is closest to conservative beliefs.

Gingrich's career has progressed side by side with the Christian Right. His belief in the possibilities of citizen-activism replacing bureaucrats dovetails with Reed's. The 1990s are a time of spiritual awakening, writes Reed:

"After the sexual revolution of the sixties, the narcissism of the seventies and the acquisitiveness of the eighties, Americans are turning inward and upward to fill what Pascal called the God-shped vacuum in every person's soul."

Reed and Gingrich share an agenda, though Reed does lace his with Scripture: Each wants to return prayer to public schools. After the Republican victories in 1994 guaranteed Gingrich the Speaker's chair, he came under fire in the press from Democrats and even from some Republicans for reiterating his long-held support for a constitutional amendment to permit voluntary prayer in schools.

The mainstream press, as a rule, subscribes to the American Civil Liberties Union positions: no public prayer and no religious symbols in public places. In a controversial lawsuit, the ACLU was able even to effect the removal of the Ten Commandments from the Cobb County courthouse, Gingrich's home base.

Moderate Republicans have criticized Gingrich for proposals that went beyond the Contract With America and perhaps put it at risk. Democrats screamed as if Gingrich were calling for the establishment of a Shiite democracy. But neither group should have been surprised.

In October, 1994, before the election, Gingrich laid out the case for a constitutional amendment in his Heritage Foundation lecture. He outlined a specific two-track strategy. The first: a bill to withdraw the issue of school prayer from court jurisdiction, a routine tactic in Congress. The second: a constitutional amendment to permit voluntary prayer. Rep. Ernest Istook of Oklahoma had been assigned to ask the Judiciary Committee to hold hearings in all 50 states by the end of June, 1995. In his lecture, Gingrich called the hearings on prayer a "forced reentry into the public debate."

He minced no words, arguing that since 1963, when the U.S. Supreme Court banned organized school prayer, "the Lyndon Johnson Great Society/McGovernite Socialist world view, combined in a sense with the Berkeley/Woodstock counterculture to argue that government bureaucracies can solve problems, that secular ways of acting are all you need." And he called the U.S. Supreme Court astonishingly ignorant.

"Why was the 1963 decision wrong? It was wrong as law because it misread the Constitution. I'm not a lawyer, but I am a historian. As an historian, I will just tell you flatly the meaning of the Constitution was simple. It was not to drive religion out of public life. It was to ensure that there would be no organized religion subsidized directly by the state and imposed on others. To attempt to interpret the language of the Constitution outside of the historical context of the late 18th century is simply stupid and should not be tolerated. People who try to do it are not engaged in an argument between two equals; they're just wrong and we ought to say that."

Gingrich got so worked up that he digressed, telling the audience he had been divorced and was remarried.

"You will have some left-wing reporter write a column about how can this hypocrite Gingrich talk about being religious, or whatever. I'm saying this because what's happened is the left has established a standard of destroying people by discovering they're human. Anybody who speaks out then becomes a hunting ground for destruction. But that's not the point of this. The point of this is to say that since all of us sin, and since all of us fall short of the glory of God, all of us need to go to God in our own way and seek God's help."

The Heritage lecture on school prayer is one of Gingrich's most powerful speeches. I suspect most listeners heard it as a cry of faith, in God and in a Republic built on the idea of God.

THE PERILS OF SOCIAL ISSUES ■ The Republican ascendancy could not have been accomplished without the Christian Coalition and the voters who agree with it. It's ironic, therefore, that after 14 years of conservative thrust on social issues, not one was part of the Contract With America. The Heritage Foundation speech gives an indication of why. Gingrich believed that to put school prayer, anti-abortion measures, affirmative action, and other "hot button" social issues front and center would provide ammunition with which a leftist press could portray the Contract's backers as radical right-wing Neanderthals.

Ralph Reed did not disagree with Gingrich's decision to defer debate in the House on the social issues. In *Politically Incorrect* and in speeches made since the elections, Reed has expanded on the "bigger tent" theory, urging religious conservatives to stress those economic and family issues on which most Americans agreed. "If religious and economic conservatives can cooperate where possible and remain civil in disagreement, they will accomplish far more together than separately."

But after the elections, when moderate, pro-choice Republicans were being mentioned for spots on the 1996 Republican ticket, Reed used a conference of young conservatives to unleash a broadside against any caviling over abortion. His adherents, he said, "will not support a party that retreats from its noble and historic defense of traditional values and which has a national ticket or a platform that does not share Ronald Reagan's belief in the sanctity of innocent human life."

Reed since has softened those remarks, but the potential problems over the issue of abortion remain. At a conference in Atlanta in April, 1995, Gingrich was asked about abortion. "I believe most Americans are pro-choice and anti-abortion." A murmur ran through the mostly conservative audience. He quieted it by insisting on putting values first in lawmaking and suggesting that alternatives to abortion such as adoption must be promoted and their costs eased. Still, the answer sounded to many like President Clinton's 1992 convention speech at which he said abortions should be "safe, legal, and rare."

Gingrich is opposed to abortion but does not believe the nation is ready to enact a constitutional ban. In the first three months of 1995, while the Contract With America was being debated, he angered some Republican congressmen by detouring them from anti-abortion amendments to bills and by putting aside their arguments that a welfare reform package might lead to an increase in abortions. The Republican side of the House is an anti-abortion group. One of the Speaker's major tests will be to manage the efforts of the pro-life representatives without seeming to be hostile. He is, after all, staging a revolution across many fronts.

Speaker Gingrich can expect attacks from both sides. The liberal assaults on his political ethics and on the alleged mean-spiritedness of Republican legislation will continue as long as he is in office. Already he is being attacked from the far right for his support of free trade and by libertarians for an interventionist foreign policy and insufficient efforts to abolish government departments. It is not likely, however, that his alliance with the Christian Coalition, the most powerful new force in American politics, will be damaged—unless a rupture occurs over abortion.

CHAPTER 10

"THEY WILL DO ANYTHING TO STOP US"

"We've had this little thing about the book. Now, I'm not going to spend a lot of time on the book, and I'm going to be very—try to always be candid.

Your chairman told me not to do it. He said it's just going to be a big distraction, a lot of noise.

Well, he's certainly right about the big distraction and lot of noise part, and maybe I shouldn't have started out to do it, but I'll tell you, I've already had three book contracts approved over the years by the Ethics Committee. There are 29 U.S. senators who have written books. I never complained. We did not run a single ad in 1992 attacking Al Gore for getting a $100,000 advance. We did not attack him a single step for making $800,000 or $900,000. We argued about the contents of his book. And so I, frankly, didn't think about it when it started.

I've had one meeting in my life with Mr. Murdoch. I had a second meeting last night, but I made sure Ted Turner and 49 other people were around me all the time. And frankly, when the folks first came to me started talking about this, I didn't think much about it except in the sense that Marianne and I are middle class, and frankly, if somebody walks by and says, 'Would you like to consider a contract for that kind of money?' we just didn't automatically say, 'Well, of course not.'

Now, I know there are important Democrats in this city who would have automatically turned down $4.5 million. They'd have said, 'I can make too much money in cattle futures.'

*I announced [for office] in April 1974 and made a
speech about cleaning up the U.S. Congress. I ran twice
and got defeated. The third time I won, I got to
Washington.*

*As a freshman, in the first six months I was here, I
made a motion to expel a member of Congress. He was a
Democratic committee chairman, he had stolen $70,000,
he was convicted on 29 felony counts, and he was still
voting.*

*We lost the vote to expel, but they changed the rules of
the House so you can't vote now when you're out on
appeal.*

*The second year, I participated in expelling a
Republican member from our conference—the first time
it was ever done—because he was involved in the Abscam
scandal and was a disgrace.*

*Three years after that, I moved to censure both a
Democrat and a Republican because they exploited pages
sexually while they were under our care. Both parties.*

*Two years after that, or three years after that, Bob
Walker and I got up and we fought over the Democratic
chairman of the Banking Committee who had been using
the credit card of a lobbyist from the savings and loan
industry, literally carrying the card around. And we
forced a fight and we fought all the way through for over
a year.*

*The following year I filed charges against the Speaker
of the House. And you can read it as recently as this
morning where there's a piece of trash in the* Washington
Post *which ends up saying the Democrats are using on
me what I used on Jim Wright. That's like saying of a
prosecutor that when the Mafia does to the prosecutor
what he did to them, they're morally equal. Jim Wright
was a crook. When they investigated Jim Wright, he had
to resign.*

*When I filed—let me just finish this out so you
understand how grotesque and disgusting I find this to
be. When I filed charges against Jim Wright, which was*

in some ways one of the loneliest and toughest days of my life, and Marianne was the one person who walked down with me to file, Bill Alexander, one of Wright's lieutenants, filed 10 charges against me and my wife. We spent $145,000 in legal fees, we were investigated for 18 months. My wife's career was literally sidetracked because she'd walk in to see somebody about a job and say, 'Oh, by the way, my husband and I are under investigation by a Congressional committee with subpoena power.'

At the end of 18 months, they not only found that every single charge was a lie, the only thing they could find me guilty of after 18 months was that I had failed to report I cosigned my daughter's house.

Now, I just want you all to think about that. That's the environment.

Barney Frank hates me. Why does Barney Frank hate me? Because when the House reported that he had lied to a parole officer on behalf of a criminal and he was reprimanded, I moved to censure him and failed. And when I see him in a newspaper talking about me being intellectually dishonest, I am sickened by a press corps that would report it.

David Bonior has never recovered from the fact that all through the mid-1980s he fought to stop aid to the contras, and I fought in favor of helping the contras, and in the end freedom won. And he has never gotten over the fact that he was on the losing side and that he doesn't get it.

Now this is where it's at. This city is going to be a mean, tough, hard city, and everybody better understand that coming down the road.

But let me tell you about the other side. Every book contract I've had went to the Ethics Committee. This book contract, when it is written—it's not even finished yet—will go to the Ethics Committee. I don't do things without going to it.

My course, Renewing American Civilization, went to

the Ethics Committee. I met with the Ethics Committee lawyers before we raised a penny. We walked through the procedures before we raised a penny. And the Democratic Chairman of the Ethics Committee knew that, and he deliberately did not inform the members of the committee.

Now what you've got in this city is a simple principle. I am a genuine revolutionary; they are the genuine reactionaries. We are going to change their world; they will do anything to stop us. They will use any tool—there is no grotesquerie, no distortion, no dishonesty too great for them to come after us.

And if you think I'm exaggerating, imagine that you're Senator Chris Dodd; you're the brand-new chairman of the Democratic National Committee. If you want to talk about ethics, you could ask why the Secretary of Commerce took money from a Brazilian businessman; you could ask why the Secretary of Agriculture had to resign because of Tyson Foods; you could ask whether or not the Secretary of HUD lied to the FBI; you could ask whether or not Ira Magaziner had lied to a Federal judge; you could ask why the Deputy Attorney General had to plead guilty to two felony counts. You have many ethics opportunities.

But for Marianne and me to have tried every way we could to be totally honest, for us to have lived on limited incomes, for us to have been scrupulous about what we've done, and then to have the news media of this city used as a tool of the Democratic Party, to just go out again and again and again, in a one-sided way, I think is a despicable comment on how sick this city got.

I want to remind all of you I turned down $4.5 million. And I'll be glad to debate any Democrat who has turned down $4.5 million about ethics. This is the amount of the advance: $1.

But I'll also tell you this. The Contract With America worked because it had ideas. I'm going to write a book. I don't know if it's going to be a good book or a bad book.

It's going to be a book about April of '97. It's going to be a book about the America that can be. It's going to be a book about the world that ought to be.

If people want to buy it, Marianne and I will probably do pretty well. If people don't want to buy it, we probably won't do very well. This is a system called free enterprise. The Socialists in the Democratic Party don't quite get it."

(Newt Gingrich, remarks to the Republican National Committee, Washington, January 20, 1995)

Gingrich gave that speech to fellow Republican political operatives against the advice of Haley Barbour, the Republican National Chairman. So many things he's said since November 4, 1994, have come against the advice of friends. He knows that hundreds of enemy torpedos are out there trying to hit him below the water line. But Gingrich lives dangerously. It's surprising for someone fond of rationalism, who measures the chances of his marriage in electoral percentages, and who constantly is figuring the odds. Newt is an oddity among politicians. What he says on the record is often much harsher than what he says for background. Chew the fat with him and you get philosophy. Put him in front of a microphone and you get a headline. Every bold, aggressive statement carries the risk of the misplaced comma or period, or the adjective that goes too far. President Clinton is "the enemy of normal Americans." "Our liberal national elite doesn't believe in religion." "It used to be called socialism; now it's just sort of liberal Democratic platform pledges."

For that sort of speech, payback can be arranged. Call a politician a thug, and you can expect the political version of a visit in a dark alley. And someone looking to defenestrate you.

"I kind of live on the edge," he told me in an interview in the spring of 1995. "I push the system." The edge is where his greatest vulnerability lies. On it is his zeal to remake the American political landscape. The danger comes in how far he goes in his drive to achieve that long-ago dream of being an old-fashioned political boss.

"The rules of how the game is played in this town were invented by the Democrats," says his high-school pal, Jackie Tillman, now working for a conservative advocacy group. "Common Cause invented political action committees in an effort to control the link between money and politics. Everything Newt is doing is being done by Democrats. He's just doing it better."

She may be right. But then, most of those Democrats, in the chummy conference rooms of the House, know better than to throw stones. Newt Gingrich nailed a Speaker of the House over a book-publishing deal. But he has had three unusual book contracts that bestir his foes. Lesser representatives have been censured, in part, because of his speechmaking. He has disparaged Gary Hart, Chuck Robb, and Ted Kennedy—tabloid lotharios all. His own life can't then be off-limits to scrutiny.

But it is money that matters. In politics, follow the money. Newt Gingrich, a man of modest tastes, sees it piling up all around him. According to the *Wall Street Journal*, the Speaker has raised $35 million for Republican causes through GOPAC and other ventures. In 1993 and 1994, he raised more than $15 million. In recent years, he has been the top GOP recipient of political action committee funds. "Newt Inc." is what more than one publication has called his organizations.

Despite the pugnacity of his speech to fellow partisans in January, 1995, Gingrich understands that his decision to live dangerously means he resides in a house filled with trap doors. Any one door—book deals, political action committees, nonprofit foundations, conflicts of interest, associates enriching themselves—could open up and plunge him into failure. He knows that. Ask him privately what happens if the Democrats are successful in arranging the appointment of a special outside counsel. He shrugs the shrug of the fatalist and says, "Who knows?"

T H E   C A S E   A G A I N S T   H I M ▪ The ethics complaints referred to the House Committee on Official

Standards and Conduct are four: That Gingrich's course constituted a political activity disguised as an academic endeavor and was improperly financed by a tax-deductible foundation; that he abused his office by allowing an auction for a book won by a publisher with business before Congress; that he accepted free time on cable television for his lectures; and that he plugged the toll-free phone number through which to order his Renewing American Civilization lecture tapes while he was speaking on the House floor.

Even people close to the Democrats' well-planned assault on Gingrich know that three of the four complaints before the Ethics Committee have little merit. Gingrich looked a bit crass in plugging his lecture tapes on the House floor, but they are distributed by a nonprofit educational foundation. (Gingrich receives no money from the course.) That his lecture series was given free airtime on Mind Extension University by Jones Intercable is, Gingrich supporters say, less offensive than the taxpayer-supported House television studio used by members to beam their messages to the folks at home.

Surprisingly, Gingrich's bitterest foes don't expect the challenge to his book-publishing contract to raise many official eyebrows. It, of course, has been the most publicized charge of the lot. And it raises the largest questions. But writing books (intellectual property) was exempted from House limits on outside income. Vice President Al Gore toured 35 cities to promote his book, *Earth in the Balance*, published in 1992. A Gore spokesman said the vice president had earned $750,000 in royalties from it through 1993. As Gingrich has said, "We didn't challenge his book, only the ideas in it."

It is difficult to describe the first charge against Gingrich because of the gray areas in House rules and the complex and overlapping nature of Gingrich's enterprises. In essence, the Speaker is accused of allowing his political action committee, GOPAC, to solicit funds for the Progress & Freedom Foundation, a nonprofit group created in part to finance Gingrich's lecture series. The issue is whether political funds were commingled with tax-deductible contributions for educational purposes and, if so, whether tax-deductible funds then used for political purposes in violation of tax law.

Internal Revenue Service regulations define unlawful political activity by tax-exempt groups to include any attempt to influence "the selection, nomination, election or appointment of any individual to Federal, State or local public office or office of a political organization..." It would be a stretch to assert, as does former Rep. Ben Jones, that the lectures were an attempt to influence the 1994 elections. They were an attempt to influence every election, but so is the every move of every representative from the time her alarm clock goes off in the morning.

The Renewing American Civilization lectures are to Gingrich, who holds a Ph.D. in history, the most important event of his career. He and cocreator Owen Roberts, a businessman and major GOPAC contributor, believe the course is an important statement about the uniquely American mission. Gingrich's closest friends helped him gather his relevant ideas into a single series of lectures. He approached Kennesaw College, a state school in his district, and was received with open arms. The course, now on hold because of the Speaker's duties, was taught for one year at Kennesaw and for two at Reinhardt College, a Methodist institution in Waleska, Georgia. For three years, the course has been taught, via satellite and for credit, at 22 colleges and universities, including the University of California at Berkeley, Tulane University, Pennsylvania State University, and Clemson University. Another 12 schools have offered it for partial credit. Academic journals such as *Lingua Franca* have given the course decent marks, although they have criticized its penchant for spotlighting successful companies and entrepreneurs who also have made financial contributions. The lectures are ideological, but they aren't necessarily partisan. Democrats who share a Gingrich point of view are made welcome. Liberals, however, are not.

EXAMINING THE CASE LAW ▪ A case involving Gingrich's confidant, Joe Gaylord, is used by Democrats to illuminate how the lectures, GOPAC, and the

Progress & Freedom Foundation might be intertwined unlawfully. Gaylord is the man closest to Gingrich. He operates as an unofficial chief of staff for the Speaker, as well as being a tactical light behind GOPAC. Federal Election Commission records show that Gaylord earned $326,000 in 1994 advising the Gingrich campaign, the National Republican Congressional Committee, and GOPAC.

In an earlier venture, Gaylord put together a tax-exempt operation called the American Campaign Academy, a school for campaign staff backed by the National Republican Congressional Committee. The U.S. Tax Court revoked the Academy's charitable status on the grounds that it served the private interests of the Republican Party rather than the public interest.

Gingrich's foes, working full-time in Washington and Georgia, call the donations by GOPAC contributors to the Progress & Freedom Foundation improper "political charity." Almost half the contributors to the foundation and its lectures are contributors to GOPAC. The critics' smoking gun is a fund-raising letter dated July, 1993, from Jeffrey Eisenach, the former executive director of GOPAC who established the Progress & Freedom Foundation. In it, he told prospective donors of the goal of the lectures, to "train 200,000-plus citizens into a model for replacing the welfare state and reforming our government." In August that year, Gingrich wrote another such letter and put it stronger terms. "Our goal," he wrote, "is to have 200,000 committed citizen activists nationwide before we're done."

Eisenach's move from GOPAC to the foundation, the fund-raising efforts of GOPAC officials, and their mass mailings are all subjects of Ethics Committee inquiry. Committee and Kennesaw State College officials maintain they weren't told of GOPAC's involvement when the course was approved.

THE SPEAKER'S RESPONSE ▪ The squad of Democratic lawyers working on the Gingrich charges maintain that the Speaker is more vulnerable to charges of wrongdoing over the tax-exempt foundation and his alleged lack of candor with the Ethics Committee than any of the other charges filed against him. Although Gingrich had obtained the committee's approval for the course, his foes say he did not alert the committee to the course's true scope: its national distribution by satellite, including gatherings far different from a small class of college students. Many of those viewing the lectures around the country were Republican groups.

For his part, Gingrich responded to the committee probe with a detailed filing in March, 1995. He and his lawyers contend that an Ethics Committee lawyer was asked specifically if course organizers paid by GOPAC need reveal their dual employment. He contends he was told dual employment wasn't a problem. His lawyer, Jan Baran, did confirm that GOPAC employees helped organize the course but maintains their efforts were ethical.

"Conclusions drawn from the fact that certain individuals inadvertently continued to use GOPAC stationery and fax machines," Baran wrote, "and that GOPAC and course organizers shared office space—which appears to be the sole basis of the complaint's allegations—are superficial and irrelevant." Who was working for whom and when will be a difficult thing to determine. Some GOPAC officials left the committee to go to work for the foundation. Others split their days. For a time, employees of both shared office space.

PLUGGING THOSE WHO PAY ▪ It is likely the charges that Gingrich plugged his contributors in the course will be swept aside. After he became Speaker, he dropped some of the commercial plugs. Two of his references, the Ford Motor Company and Southwire, were naturals for Newt.

Gingrich's original Sixth District had just a few large employers. Both Ford and Southwire have figured into Gingrich's career. The Ford Motor Company plant in Hapeville, a blue-collar town next to Atlanta's Hartsfield International Airport, is one of Gingrich's favorite examples of successful management. It was near extinction, a troubled unit of a troubled company, until Ford reinvented itself. Gingrich has devoted large portions of his lectures to how Ford followed the advice of the management guru, W. Edwards Deming, and led the recovery of the U.S. auto industry. The Hapeville facility became the major manufacturer of the Taurus, the model that topped the Honda Accord as the biggest-selling car in the U.S., and is rated one of the most efficient auto plants in the world. In April, 1995, upon completion of the first 100 days of the new Congress, Gingrich singled Ford out for praise in a nationally televised address. The other major employer, Southwire, in Carrollton, has caused Gingrich several kinds of troubles. During his unsuccessful congressional campaigns in 1974 and 1976, the environmentalist Gingrich was critical of Southwire, accusing it of pollution. At the time, the firm's founder, Roy Richards, dominated west Georgia. His family owned the Carrollton newspaper and the bank, among other holdings.

Roy Richards made small contributions to Gingrich, but reserved the larger dollars for Gingrich's opponent, Jack Flynt. After Gingrich won office, the Richards family became major supporters, and its contributions to Gingrich enterprises over the years exceed $100,000. As with many industrial firms, Southwire has had its problems with the government and has been fined many times for environmental violations. At one of his daily press conferences in February, 1995, Gingrich was asked by a reporter how he could take contributions from a company that had been found guilty of criminal violations of environmental law.

"You're talking about the biggest employer in Carroll County," he replied. "And you know, I fully support the federal government prosecuting companies when they break the law. But I hardly think that, given the complexity of our environmental and OSHA regulations, that having been convicted of a violation turns one into a criminal company, as you describe it. They are good citizens. They work very hard. They provide very good jobs for over three thousand people."

Another contributor singled out for praise in the lectures is Roger Milliken, who built Milliken Industries, the innovative textile giant. He and his brother, Gerrish, have given $345,000 to GOPAC. But when Roger Milliken was opposing the North American Free Trade Agreement, his money carried little weight. Gingrich orchestrated the Republican support needed to help President Clinton pass the bill over the objections of labor unions and protectionist Democrats. Milliken also opposed the General Agreement on Tariffs and Trade, or GATT. Foes of the tariff treaty ran radio commercials in Atlanta in which Pat Buchanan urged constituents to call or write Gingrich in opposition ("Congressman Gin-rich," he called him). Gingrich was unmoved and voted for GATT.

My personal favorite is Norman Brinker, a self-made man who founded the Steak and Ale restaurant chain and is credited with inventing the restaurant salad bar. He is the subject of extended video treatment in the lectures, which foes contend is an ethical violation. Gingrich told me he has never met him.

Less weighty matters also await the committee's attention. Critics have charged that Gingrich used staffers from his House office to work on the course, a violation of House rules and of a specific warning from the Ethics Committee in granting its approval of the course. Those stories have led to recitations of past accounts of Gingrich's use of his congressional staff for political work and in campaigns. Most such accounts simply dust off the reporting of Michael Hinkelman in the *Atlanta Business Chronicle* years ago that had been used by his opponents in campaigns.

"He does the same things he made a career out of attacking Democrats on," says Gingrich's two-time opponent, Dave Worley. "And every time he has an idea, he gathers a group of wealthy supporters to underwrite it."

DIGGING DEEP FOR GOPAC ▪ A problem that has consistently dogged Gingrich (and has now been partially corrected) is that early GOPAC contributions weren't disclosed by amounts or donors. GOPAC officials maintained the funds weren't used for federal candidates, making federal reporting unnecessary. Also, partial disclosure and press leaks have revealed contributions larger than are usually received by candidates. They are of the size made to national political parties in what is known as "soft money" for party election expenses.

Terry and Mary Kohler of Wisconsin, for instance, have contributed $738,457 to Gingrich campaigns and GOPAC over the years. The Kohlers are interested in conservative ideas, but the amounts and numbers of contributions give even Gingrich allies pause for concern over possible future conflicts of interest or preferential treatment. Owen Roberts of Florida, the investment counselor and futurist who helped devise the lecture series, has contributed $336,513 to Gingrich's reelection and to GOPAC. And after the 1994 elections, money flowed into GOPAC and into Gingrich's Progress & Freedom Foundation. Critics say that since campaign contributions are limited by law, the huge contributions to GOPAC amount to breaking the rules by circumventing them through the huge payments to the political action committee and the nonprofit foundation. Gingrich allies respond that political action committees are a staple of business in today's Washington.

For all the headlines, none of the money seems to have yet found its way into the Speaker's pockets. He lives still in a small home in suburban Atlanta and a tiny rental apartment near Capitol Hill. He still owns a 1967 Mustang, and his taste in restaurants is modest and predictable. His disclosure forms show he has accumulated next to nothing for a man past 50 who's the father of two. (All that might change if his HarperCollins book sells well.)

SPOUSES IN THE SPOTLIGHT ▪ Any legitimate ethical issues that might be discussed about "Newt Inc." seem lost in the mud-against-the-wall attacks of the Democrats. The strategy of the Atlanta and Washington lawyers working the case and much of the press coverage seems to be to turn over rocks and sling mud— often out-of-context mud—until enough of it sticks to the doors of the Ethics Committee and forces Chairman Nancy Johnson of

Connecticut to agree to an outside special counsel. For so often, independent counsels start out investigating one thing and end up turning over a rock hidden somewhere else. They can investigate contributions to a college course and uncover illegal payments to the college basketball team. Gingrich knows that he doesn't know everything about his far-flung political and educational enterprises.

This is not to suggest that he or his machine has engaged in illegal or unethical behavior. But his focus on the permanent campaign may have stripped him of the time needed to be wary. The House ethics rules are in a book with hundreds of pages. Potential violations occur with every footnote, especially in anything involving the Internal Revenue Service. On the flip side, however, some of the complaints against him are so laughable they could be parodied by "Saturday Night Live" (back when the program had a sense of humor).

The Speaker's chief critic, Minority Whip David Bonior of Michigan, sounds at times like the Gingrich of old. He says of the Republicans: "They just think they're the almighty. It shows their arrogance. They have the sense they're above the law." His goal is plain: "To regain the House of Representatives by showing the bankruptcy of the Speaker himself in respect to these ethical issues."

But Bonior, still angry at Gingrich's attacks on him for his support of the Sandinista government of Nicaragua, can be petty. Take, for instance, the charge that Gingrich violated House rules by promoting his lectures on the House floor and on C-Span. Bonior notes that because the remarks were reprinted in the *Congressional Record*, supported by the taxpayers, they might violate House rules against using public resources to solicit for a private foundation.

Gingrich accepts that some of these ethical questions involve substantive issues, but he bristles at what he considers pettiness. He grows angry at any mention of the criticisms leveled at his wife, Marianne. After he was chosen Speaker, Marianne was hired by the Israel Export Development Company to help lure businesses to a free-trade zone. The job was called a political payoff in return for Gingrich's advocacy of the free-trade zone to Israeli officials. Critics contended it was a conflict of interest for the Speaker and that since Marianne works primarily on commission, the appearance of potential conflict arises with every deal that's made. The same can be said of Newt's fund-raising empire. Most political campaign contributions from businesses aren't made simply for ideological reasons. Most executives are pragmatic and want something from their representatives. In Gingrich's case, opposed as he is to higher taxes and expansive regulations, businesses gravitate to him. When he answers a request for a favor for a constituent, is it always a case of improper influence? Or is it simply a responsive, politically attuned representative with an attentive staff?

As a result of the hue and cry, Marianne now is working up a bipartisan task force of congressional spouses to seek a review of House ethics standards on what jobs are allowable for spouses. The conflict-of-interest question deserves resolution in an era in which more and more representatives' spouses are likely to have careers of their own.

THE $4.5 MILLION AUTHOR ▪ Less than two weeks before being sworn in as Speaker, Gingrich agreed to a two-book deal with HarperCollins, the publishing house owned by Rupert Murdoch and his News Corp. With an advance against sales of $4.5 million, it was one of the most lucrative payouts ever for a political book and unprecedented for a sitting member of the House. In fact, the deal had been in the works for months, well before almost anyone but Newt Gingrich and Joe Gaylord thought the GOP would win the House.

Gingrich loves books. He always carries one or two wherever he goes, in case there's a lull in the action and he can catch up. He would love to write a bestseller, not so much for the pleasures of a writer's contemplative life but for the credence it would give his ideas.

Books have put him into hot frying pans before. In 1977, a dozen wealthy backers put together $13,000 to allow him to write the great American novel. At the time, Gingrich was broke and a two-time loser in politics. Having failed to seek tenure at West Georgia College, he was soon to be out of a job. The deal was a tax shelter for the investors, an issue opponent Dave Worley would take up many years later, suggesting the investors sought favor and influence from a future member of Congress. Gingrich used some of the money to take his family to Europe. He eventually finished the work, a novel about World War III, but was discouraged about its prospects by friends such as author Alvin Toffler and fellow historian Steve Hanser. The book was never published.

In 1989, when Gingrich was attacking Speaker Jim Wright's book deal, Gingrich critics brought up Gingrich's own book (then five years old), *Window Of Opportunity*. With Marianne, the congressman had created a limited partnership to promote the book after publication. Twenty-one supporters kicked in $5,000 each. The title lists Marianne as coauthor, but she also was paid to be general manager of the limited partnership. Gingrich believed that promotion funds and exposure at the 1984 Republican Convention could create a bestseller. The flap over that book's financing led to a memorable Washington press conference held by the couple; Marianne was there in her role as the businessperson who arranged the deal. The questioning of Newt became so raucous that she fled in tears.

In 1994, Gingrich's agent, Lynn Chu, began circulating proposals for a new Gingrich book. She found enough interest to suggest conducting an auction among publishers. Gingrich liked the blind bid idea, for it removed some potential for a conflict of interest. One other publishing house exceeded $4 million before HarperCollins made its winning bid. In *To Renew America*, with a tentative publication date of fall, 1995, Gingrich will outline his plans for the future of the nation. He will then prepare an anthology of historical essays on America and write an introduction and commentary.

The Speaker was wide-eyed over the deal. Like many middle-aged men with responsibilities, he was looking down the road to retirement with little else than a government pension (albeit the lavish one accorded congressmen). When the criticism began, he was at first defiant, telling the *Wall Street Journal*, "Conservative books sell. I can't help it if liberal books don't sell."

He trumpeted his triumph in the free market and argued that the interest of major publishers validated his ideas. But the criticism escalated. Conservative commentators joined the partisan critics. For the public, it was too much. Few know that book royalties are exempted from congressional rules limiting outside income.

The deal with HarperCollins had two major problems in addition to the size of the author's advance. First was the perception that Gingrich had used the election victories and his sudden high profile to capitalize on his office even before he had taken the oath. David Bonior called it a "$4 million Christmas gift." Second was the realization that Rupert Murdoch had multimillion-dollar issues before Congress. He has been in a huge struggle with the Federal Communications Commission over whether his many American television stations are owned by him, an American citizen, or his News Corp., an Australian company. U.S. law forbids foreign ownership of broadcast licenses. A few Republicans in Congress were already pushing for deregulation of broadcasting that would have allowed Murdoch and others to expand. Murdoch had paid a courtesy visit to Gingrich after the 1994 elections. Both men said no broadcasting issues or book contracts were discussed.

In the week between Christmas, 1994, and New Year's Day, 1995, Gingrich reached out to friends for advice. Some suggested that Murdoch, more than the large advance, was the problem and that Gingrich should gracefully leave HarperCollins in favor of the second bidder. Others urged him to give up the idea all together. Gingrich finally reached a compromise: He would forego all but $1 of the advance. He would leave the cushion of the celebrity advance guarantee for a gamble on the free market. Gingrich is to earn a standard 15 percent royalty from sales. The terms of the book contract, submitted to the Ethics Committee, are essentially the same as those that Vice President Gore received for *Earth in the Balance*.

CASHING IN TOO EARLY? ▪ Few question that the book deal damaged the Speaker's standing. Before the House convenes each day, members line up for a series of one-minute speeches. Rare is the day when at least one Democrat doesn't mention the book deal and contrast it with reduced increases in spending for the poor.

When the Ethics Committee got the contract, it also learned that Gingrich was working on several additional book projects. He has contracted to write four novels for Baen Publishing. Democrats have begun to attack the deals on the grounds that such a workload must take away from his duties.

In a conversation with Gingrich in March of 1995, I asked him when, with his taxing schedule, he could find the time, even with coauthors, to write one book—let alone six.

"Saturday afternoons," he said. Seriously? "Yes, I try to reserve that time to stick to the laptop." When Congress went into recess after its first 100 days, Gingrich blocked out a month with only one scheduled public event per day. The rest of his time was reserved for writing.

Though Gingrich has deflected some of the criticism from the HarperCollins contract by giving up a check for $4.5 million, the issues remain open. Books certainly are intellectual property for congressmen, engaged in what should be a thoughtful profession. But the changing nature of the publishing industry, with its increasingly large advances, points to a need to prevent representatives from growing rich on the public payroll. As the conservative columnist for the *New York Times*, William Safire, put it so succinctly, "Wait until retirement to cash in." Gingrich could win back some luster by proposing a rules change to see to it that book contracts don't carry the appearance of a payoff for celebrity or for favors.

Murdoch, for the record, did benefit from congressional action. In January, 1995, Republicans in the House moved to strike a 17-year-old preference in broadcast law that allowed station and cable system owners to defer capital gains from the sale of a property if it were sold to minorities. Murdoch's Fox Television Stations division was trying to sell its WATL-TV in Atlanta to a minority group financed by the Chicago Tribune Company. He stood to defer some $30 million in taxes through the sale. After the House killed the program, an exemption for Murdoch and the Tribune Company was inserted in the Senate bill by Sen. Carol Moseley Braun of Illinois. Her amendment was approved in a House-Senate conference committee. Gingrich said he was opposed to the amendment and wanted the program abolished altogether, but the House was powerless to negotiate the one exemption away. In addition, the measure was tied to a Republican promise to allow self-employed people to deduct part of the cost of their health insurance. President Clinton said he would refuse to veto the bill for much the same reason—it was a sound measure overall.

As long as Gingrich is on the attack and as long as he pushes the envelope of the House rules on fundraising and foundations, he will be dogged by ethical complaints. His foes are determined that his house be exposed as glass. But the severity of the current criticism was lessened considerably in April, 1995, when the *Washington Post* argued in an editorial that "an independent counsel or other type of outside adviser or arbiter is neither warranted nor required by what is known." The *Post*, the voice of the Washington establishment, argued that the Ethics Committee should make the tough choices and look hard at new rules to clarify the many gray areas of contributions, appearances of conflicts of interest, and sources of outside income.

Gingrich still could face an independent counsel or a scolding or censure by the Ethics Committee. Its members, however, are aware that Gingrich's activities are neither new nor the sole province of Republicans. Political action committees, labor unions, and other special interests play the same game on the Democratic side of the aisle. The more likely outcome is that the Speaker will be found guilty of playing the game harder and more effectively than his foes, and using the rules to best advantage.

BEYOND 100 DAYS

"You have to blow down the old
order in order to create the new
order."

BEYOND
100 DAYS

*"I still believe in a very activist government. I just think it
has to be narrowly defined. I'd like the government to be
extraordinarily activist in crushing the drug trade. I'm for
space exploration and doing biological surveys and a
whole range of things. In terms of research and
development for education, I think government can be
very activist. I just think that as a deliverer of ongoing
continuous services, it is tragically incompetent and prone
to corruption. But you wouldn't have a computer
industry or a private jet aircraft industry without
government. And the transcontinental railroad and the
Panama Canal."*

(Newt Gingrich, interview, April, 1995)

When Newt Gingrich went to Washington as a rookie
congressman in 1979, a poster unusual for Washington
adorned his office wall. At the time, Gingrich was the only
Republican representing Georgia on Capitol Hill, so most of
the guests at his office-warming were Democrats. The visitors
buzzed at what Gingrich possibly could mean by displaying
the poster for the movie, "The Candidate," starring Robert
Redford. Did he see himself as the handsome film star? Didn't
he know Redford played a good-looking empty suit who ran
at the mercy of his handlers?

Gingrich knew that and more. With his girth, he's no

Redford, nor did he want to be the character Redford played. In the film's memorable last scene, after Redford has won a U.S. Senate seat, he turns to his aides and asks, "What do we do now?" Gingrich has never forgotten that line. "I put it [the poster] there to remind me what I didn't want to become," he told me in a recent interview.

Gingrich knows what's next. His vision of an opportunity society hasn't yet become reality. The strategy is still being executed. The next set of projects and tactics awaits the next meeting of the next congressional committee.

Many a person would rest on the laurels of the first 100 days of the 104th Congress, basking in the congratulations and the opinion polls that showed a majority of Americans believed the Republican majority had done a good job. Others might simply have collapsed from exhaustion. In April, 1995, Gingrich could have been forgiven ratcheting back his punishing schedule. After all, he had led the House to passage of nine of the 10 items in the Contract With America. He requested and was given time on national television for a speech to the nation at the end of the 100 days, an unprecedented event for a Speaker. The more deliberative U.S. Senate was being criticized for not keeping up with the House's legislative pace. His Democratic foes were dispirited and divided. The question many were asking about President Clinton was, is he relevant? Newt Gingrich's vision, strategy, projects, and tactics had made the House of Representatives the dominant power center in Washington.

Gingrich didn't take a vacation. Instead he went home to Georgia and pushed himself at his computer, turning out thousands of words each day to fulfill his major book contract, the work called *To Renew America*. And before the 100 days were up, he had set forth the model for the rest of 1995. It resides in a 134-page briefing book called "The House Republican Plan for a Better America." After the House performance on the Contract With America, who would bet against his success?

CONTRACT SCORECARD ▪ After 100 days, all

10 items on the Contract had been voted on as promised.
Nine were passed and sent to the Senate.

FISCAL RESPONSIBILITY: The House passed a constitutional amendment requiring a balanced federal budget, only to
see it fall one vote short of passage in the Senate. Majority
Leader Bob Dole is likely to bring it up again before the 1996
presidential campaign. Both bodies passed a bill giving the
president the authority to veto individual budget items. The
line-item veto, given to a Democratic chief executive, was a
victory of principle over politics. The major battle ahead is the
budget for the coming years. Gingrich will attempt to slow the
growth of federal spending enough to put the budget into
balance by the year 2002.

TAXES: The House, with 27 Democrats in support, passed a
bill for a $500 tax credit to families for each child under 18
years of age. Another credit eased the so-called marriage
penalty, which taxes a married couple at a higher rate than a
man and woman filing separately. The bill featured exclusions
of some capital gains from taxes; a new form of Individual
Retirement Account allowing for withdrawals for education,
medical expenses, and first-time home purchases; and repeal
of the 1993 tax increase on Social Security recipients. The bill
faces rough going in the Senate, where ranking Republicans
would rather see the deficit reduced than pass a tax cut.

WELFARE REFORM: House Republicans sustained heavy
political damage in the debate over the bill to dismantle 45
federal social programs and send the money to the states in
the form of block grants. Democrats called the provisions
mean-spirited spending cuts. The Republicans argued that
spending increased, though not at the rate Democrats wanted.
States, they believe, can handle the programs more efficiently.
The bill also prohibits cash benefits to teenaged mothers and
limits increases to mothers who have additional children while
on welfare. Its most controversial feature is a two-year limit
on benefits and a work requirement. President Clinton doesn't

believe the bill goes far enough to require work by welfare recipients.

FAMILY REINFORCEMENT: The House passed tougher provisions to collect child support from parents, tax incentives for adoptions, and a variety of measures to protect children and involve their parents in their education.

CRIME: A six-part crime measure would send $10 billion to local governments. In 1994, Congress passed President Clinton's bill to send money from Washington to allow the hiring of 100,000 new policemen across the nation. The House in 1995 changed the funds to block grants, with wider local discretion for their use. The House also passed "truth-in-sentencing," requiring inmates to serve a higher proportion of their terms, the "good faith" exemption in the exclusionary rule on police searches, and limits on appeals in death-penalty cases.

LITIGATION REFORM: The House limited the ability of consumers to win damage awards in product-liability cases against manufacturers and capped punitive damages in state and federal civil suits.

REGULATORY REFORM: Both houses passed a ban on unfunded mandates, those federal regulations imposed on states and local governments without accompanying federal funds. House Republicans also passed a moratorium on all new federal regulations.

NATIONAL SECURITY: Under a measure passed by the House, no U.S. troops can be placed under the command of the United Nations. With both houses moving toward a balanced budget by the year 2002, cuts in the growth of defense spending are likely.

CONGRESSIONAL REFORM: In the marathon opening day of the 104th Congress, the House passed legislation requiring

Congress to abide by the same labor laws it imposes on the private sector. President Clinton signed it into law. In addition, Speaker Gingrich cut congressional committees by a third, reduced staff, and did away with special-interest caucuses that operated outside the House and party structures.

TERM LIMITS: The only item in the Contract With America not to receive House passage was the constitutional amendment to limit how long lawmakers could serve. To fulfill the Contract promise, several proposals were voted on, but none received the two-thirds majority necessary for a constitutional amendment. Gingrich noted that 85 percent of Republicans voted for term limits, compared to only 15 percent of the Democrats. He vowed to make it the first bill considered by the next Congress.

GOOD REVIEWS ▪ Many Contract items will be watered down or eliminated in the Senate. Others may be vetoed by President Clinton. But polls indicated that voters liked the accountability shown by the majority Republicans. In 100 days, they struck a blow at the notion of Washington gridlock. Said Thomas Mann of the Brookings Institution: "It is democratic accountability at its best."

Other reviews of his performance were just as flattering. The *New York Times* swallowed hard in an editorial attacking the Contract and said, "As a political feat, it's hard not to be impressed with—or jealous of—the single-minded unity of the Republican Congress so far. Whatever else you say about Gingrich & Co., they have quickly destroyed the myth that the House is a hopeless den of squabble, so divided by disparate interests that it is ungovernable and unable to govern. Gingrich has proved that the trouble wasn't the Congress; it was the Foleys and Rostenkowskis of the Congress. They were well dispatched."

The *Washington Post* found a good deal to like in the Republican effort: "In their first few months in office, the House Republicans have reinvigorated what had become a tired arm of national government and set a standard of boldness in the use of political power that will likely be invoked in judging new administrations and Congresses for years to come. Too often the cautious view in recent years has been that political leaders risk exhausting their political capital when they spend it. Speaker Gingrich & Co. have provided a useful reminder in a timid age that the opposite can also be true. They have spent political capital and been strengthened by it."

After the first 100 days, without the discipline imposed by the Contract With America, the road will develop more potholes. House Republicans and conservative voters likely will be frustrated with the pace and compromise of the Senate. The 1996 presidential campaign will slowly but surely overshadow the legislative branch. Social-issue and religious conservatives will want their turn at the plate—on abortion, school prayer, and the like. Fissures surely will result between them and moderate Republicans.

Gingrich has likened his role in those internal debates to the way Franklin D. Roosevelt managed his even more unlikely Democratic coalition, with its blacks, northern liberals, and southern segregationists.

"The job of political leadership," Gingrich told reporters in April, "is to manage the dialogue in such a way that the coalition holds together."

THE MORAL IMPERATIVE ■ Even as the Contract With America was being debated in February and March, Gingrich had turned his attention to the federal budget. In an interview with me in March, he outlined his strategy. "We have to have new ideas larger than the other side has objections," he said.

The momentum has been growing to replace the federal income tax with Rep. Dick Armey's flat-rate tax with few deductions or Rep. Bill Archer's sales tax at every level of distribution. Gingrich and Dole selected Jack Kemp to head a commission to study reform of the tax system. The commission signals Republican intentions to have a major national debate on what once was unthinkable: eliminating the progressive income tax and maybe even the Internal Revenue Service.

By far the biggest issue facing Congress is the budget deficit. Gingrich casts it in moral terms, calling it a moral imperative to reduce the debt load of future generations. A child born in 1995, he says, will pay $187,150 over her lifetime just in interest on the debt building over her lifetime. In his view, it would be immoral not to put the budget on the path toward balance in 2002.

"I regard getting to the balanced budget as the fulcrum to move the whole system," he said in an interview for this book. "It's the only thing that gives you the moral imperative to change the whole structure of the welfare state. By balancing the budget, the Republicans will be protecting children, baby-boomers, and senior citizens."

He turned to the Duke of Wellington for advice in the budget battle, studying how the outmanned British commander defeated Napoleon in the Peninsula Campaign in Spain and Portugal in 1813. A series of nearly impregnable defensive positions wore down the French armies. Gingrich's defensive positions will be each area of federal spending, particularly the $305 billion a year he attributes to social welfare programs. He and his colleagues will challenge the Democrats to justify every dollar spent, wearing them into submission.

"The only battle that matters is the budget," he said in an April interview for this book. "From now until November is Wellington's Peninsula campaign. It's so bold that if we don't lose, we may win."

Don't confuse the Gingrich of 1995 with Ronald Reagan of 1980, when the president cut the growth of federal spending and lowered taxes. Gingrich wants to prune the government so it can be redirected: "You did not have in the Reagan team the ability to create a sophisticated positive view of governance, which I'm trying to do now. You have to blow down the old order in order to create the new order. Reagan understood how to blow down the old order, but wasn't exactly sure what the new order would be. The Bush people were too timid to blow down the old order."

The new order, of course, would be the opportunity society. Gingrich calls it "truly compassionate," unlike the welfare state that traps people in poverty, stifles innovation, holds back economic growth and puts children at risk through the oppressive national debt they inherit.

One sure measure of Gingrich's impact since November, 1994, is the reaction of Democrats. President Clinton has asked cabinet officers to produce savings and eliminate programs. Democrats even have gone so far as to suggest abolishing some cabinet-level federal departments. Both Clinton and House Minority Leader Richard Gephardt have suggested tax cuts (though Gephardt opposed the Republican version that passed the House).

Newt Gingrich, with ideas newer and bigger than the Democrats are offering, is setting the agenda and, to use his words, managing the dialogue.

In political terms, the Republican tide of 1994 did not ebb the following year. Two senators, Richard Shelby of Alabama and Ben Nighthorse Campbell of Colorado, and one representative, Nathan Deal of Georgia, made it 78 local, state, and federal officials who have become Republicans since Bill Clinton was elected president. The political map looks like a reversal of the map from New Deal days. The 104th Congress is the first since Reconstruction with a Republican majority of the 125 seats in the states of the Confederacy, the once–Solid South.

The Speaker has proven he can direct a national campaign and manage the House. In his words, he is "managing three or four revolutions at once." His political efforts to elect more Republicans are likely to intensify. So is his power in the House. When he campaigned in 127 districts, he built a file of IOUs. When he ignored seniority in choosing House Committee chairs he became a veritable central bank for loyalty.

Still, the power of the Republican tide is by no means defined. After all, most voters had never heard of the Contract With America when they cast ballots in 1994. Public judgment on Gingrich was slow in coming; after the 100 days, he remained less popular than Clinton and the Congress he prodded into action. Bill Clinton has come back from defeat and misfortune several times in his career and could well seize on a strong economy and Republican divisions to win reelection in 1996.

Nothing that happens in 1996, however, can take away from the accomplishments of Gingrich in his long march to leader of the majority. Irving Kristol, the neo-conservative editor of *The Public Interest*, has seen the shifts of power in this century; he captured the Gingrich era in an article for the *Washington Post*:

"The American people now have a Republican Party that is future-oriented, rather than 'conservative' in the older stick-in-the-mud meaning of the term. One need not take too seriously Newt Gingrich's 'futuristic' speculations to appreciate the importance of this change. From having been a party of resistance to the liberal agenda, the Republican Party is now preparing to be the governing party with its own agenda. And in a modern democracy, integrated into a dynamic world economy, with a high degree of individual liberty and individual mobility, any succcessful conservative party has to be (a) future oriented in its economic and social agenda while (b) retaining powerful links to traditional moral and cultural values."

Gingrich's unlikely rise from the army meritocracy of his childhood through the political transformation of the conservative South positions him to lead the Republicans in the direction Kristol suggests.

When the 100 days ended, Newt Gingrich brought the Ringling Brothers Barnum and Bailey circus to the U.S. Capitol and seemed literally to dance with the elephants. To look back on his unlikely career is to see a man born to tame these largest of beasts and stick around to lead the parade. Only the foolish will laugh. For Gingrich knows that elephants are the symbol of the long-term strategy. They never forget.

As Republican Members of the House of Representatives and as citizens seeking to join that body we propose not just to change its policies, but even more important, to restore the bonds of trust between the people and their elected representatives. That is why, in this era of official evasion and posturing, we offer instead a detailed agenda for national renewal, a written commitment with no fine print.

This year's election offers the chance, after four decades of one-party control, to bring to the House a new majority that will transform the way Congress works. That historic change would be the end of government that is too big, too intrusive, and too easy with the public's money. It can be the beginning of a Congress that respects the values and shares the faith of the American family.

Like Lincoln, our first Republican president, "with firmness in the right, as God gives us to see the right." To restore acountability to Congress. To end its cycle of scandal and disgrace. To make us all proud again of the way free people govern themselves.

On the first day of the 104th Congress, the new Republican majority will immediately pass the following major reforms, aimed at restoring the faith and trust of the American people in their government:

First, require that all laws that apply to the rest of the country also apply equally to the Congress;

Second, select a major independent auditing firm to conduct a comprehensive audit of Congress for waste, fraud or abuse;

Third, cut the number of House committees, and cut committee staff by one-third;

Fourth, limit the terms of all committee chairs;

Fifth, ban the casting of proxy votes in committee;

Sixth, require committee meetings to be open to the public;

Seventh, require a three-fifths majority vote to pass a tax increase;

Eighth, guarantee an honest accounting of our federal budget by implementing zero baseline budgeting.

Thereafter, within the first 100 days of the 104th Congress, we shall bring to the House floor the following bills, each to be given full and open debate, each to be given a clear and fair vote, and each to be immediately available this day for public inspection and scrutiny.

THE FISCAL RESPONSIBILITY ACT ▪ A balanced budget/tax limitation amendment and a legislative line-item veto to restore fiscal responsibility to an out-of-control Congress, requiring them to live under the same budget constraints as families and businesses.

THE TAKING BACK OUR STREETS ACT ▪ An anti-crime package including stronger truth in sentencing, "good faith" exclusionary rule exemptions, effective death penalty provisions, and cuts in social spending from this summer's crime bill to fund prison construction and additional law enforcement to keep people secure in their neighborhoods and kids safe in their schools.

THE PERSONAL RESPONSIBILITY ACT ▪ Discourage illegitimacy and teen pregnancy by prohibiting welfare to minor mothers and denying increased AFDC for additional children while on welfare, cut spending for welfare programs, and enact a tough two-years-and-out provision with work requirements to promote individual responsibility.

THE FAMILY REINFORCEMENT ACT ▪ Child support enforcement, tax incentives for adoption, strengthening rights of parents in their children's education, stronger child pornography laws, and an elderly dependent care tax credit to reinforce the central role of families in American society.

THE AMERICAN DREAM RESTORATION ACT ■ A $500-per-child tax credit, begin repeal of the marriage penalty, and creation of American Dream Savings Accounts to provide middle-class tax relief.

THE NATIONAL SECURITY RESTORATION ACT ■ No U.S. troops under UN command and restoration of the essential parts of our national security funding to strengthen our national defense and maintain our credibility around the world.

THE SENIOR CITIZENS FAIRNESS ACT ■ Raise the Social Security earnings limit, which currently forces seniors out of the work force, repeal the 1993 tax hikes on Social Security benefits, and provide tax incentives for private long-term care insurance to let older Americans keep more of what they have earned over the years.

THE JOB CREATION AND WAGE ENHANCEMENT ACT ■ Small business incentives, capital gains cut and indexation, neutral cost recovery, risk assessment/cost benefit analysis, strengthening of the Regulatory Flexibility Act, and unfunded mandate reform to create jobs and raise worker wages.

THE COMMON SENSE LEGAL REFORMS ACT ■ "Loser pays" laws, reasonable limits on punitive damages, and reform of product liability laws to stem the endless tide of litigation.

THE CITIZEN LEGISLATURE ACT ■ A first-ever vote on term limits to replace career politicians with citizen legislators.

Further, we will instruct the House Budget Committee to

report to the floor and we will work to enact additional budget savings, beyond the budget cuts specifically included in the legislation described above, to ensure that the federal budget will be less than it would have been without the enactment of these bills.

Respecting the judgment of our fellow citizens as we seek their mandate for reform, we hereby pledge our names to this *Contract With America.*

Remarks of Hon. Newt Gingrich, January 4, 1995, upon being sworn in as Speaker of the 104th Congress

....This is an historic moment. I was asked over and over again how did it feel and the only word that comes close to adequate is overwhelming. I feel overwhelmed in every way. Overwhelmed by all the Georgians who came up, overwhelmed by my extended family that is here. Overwhelmed by the historic moment I walked out and stood on the balcony just outside the Speaker's office looking down the Mall this morning very early....Just the sense of being part of America, and being part of this great tradition....

We're starting the 104th Congress. I don't know if you've ever thought about the concept: 208 years. We gather together. The most diverse country in the history of the world. We send all sorts of people. Each of us could find at least one member we thought was weird, and I tell ya', if you went around the room, the person you chose to be weird would be different for virtually every one of us.

Because we do allow, and insist upon, the right of a free people, to send an extraordinary diversity of people here. Brian Lamb of C-Span read to me Friday a phrase from de Tocqueville that was so central to the House. I've been reading [a] biography of Henry Clay, and Henry Clay always preferred the House. He was the first strong Speaker. He preferred the House to the Senate although he served in both. But he said the House was more vital, more active, more dynamic, more common.

This is what de Tocqueville wrote: "Often, there's not a distinguished man in the whole number. Its members are almost all obscure individuals, whose names bring no associations to mind. They are mostly village lawyers, men in trade, or even persons belonging to the lower classes of society."....

And so, here we are as commoners together. To some extent Democrats and Republicans, to some extent liberals and conservatives, but Americans all. Steve Gunderson today gave me a copy of the portable Abraham Lincoln, and suggested there is much for me to learn about our party. But I would also say, as I have since the election, it doesn't hurt to have a copy of the portable FDR....

Today we had a bipartisan prayer service. Frank Wolf made some very important points. He said we have to recognize that many of our most painful problems as a country are moral problems, problems of dealing with ourselves and with life. He said character is the key to leadership. He preached a little bit—I don't think he thought it was preaching, but it was— about a spirit of reconciliation. And he talked about caring about our spouses, and our children, and our families. Because if we're not prepared to model that, beyond just having them here for one day, if we're not prepared to care about our children, and we're not prepared to care about our families, then by what arrogance do we think we will transcend our behavior to care about others?

That's why, with Congressman [Richard] Gephardt's help, we've established a bipartisan task force on the family. We've established the principle that we're going to set schedules we stick to so families can count on times to be together, built around the school schedules, so that families can get to know each other. And not just on C-Span....

This may seem particularly appropriate to say on the first day because this will be the busiest day on opening day in

Congressional history. I want to read just a part of the Contract With America, not as a partisan act but to remind all of us of what we're about to go through and why.

Because those of us who ended up in a majority stood on these steps and signed a Contract, and here's part of what it says: "On the first day of the 104th Congress, the new Republican majority will immediately pass the following major reforms aimed at restoring the faith and trust of the American people in their Government. First, require all laws that apply to the rest of the country also apply equally to the Congress. Second, select a major independent auditing firm to conduct a comprehensive audit of Congress for waste, fraud, or abuse. Third, cut the number of House committees and cut committee staffs by a third. Fourth, limit the terms of all committee chairs. Fifth, ban the casting of proxy votes in committees. Sixth, require committee meetings to be open to the public. Seventh, require a three-fifths majority vote to pass a tax increase. Eighth, guarantee an honest accounting of our Federal budget by implementing zero baseline budgeting..."

Now, I told Dick last night that if I had to do it over again we would have pledged within three days we will do these things. But that's not what we said. So we got ourselves in a little bit of a box.

But then, to go a step further—I carry the *TV Guide* version of the Contract with me at all times—we then said "Thereafter, within the first 100 days of the 104th Congress we shall bring to the House floor the following bills. Each to be given full and open debate. Each to be given a clear and fair vote, and each to be immediately available for inspection." To be made available that day. And we listed 10 items:

A balanced budget amendment and line-item veto. To stop violent criminals emphasizing, among other things, an effective, enforceable death penalty. Third was welfare reform. Fourth was protecting our kids. Fifth was tax cuts for families.

Sixth was a stronger national defense. Seventh was raising the senior citizen's earning limit. Eighth was rolling back government regulation. Ninth was common-sense legal reform. And tenth was Congressional term limits.

Now, our commitment on our side, and I think we have this absolute obligation, is first of all to work today until we're done. And that I know is going to inconvenience people; there are families and supporters. But we were hired to do a job, and we have to start today to prove we'll do it....

Beyond the Contract, I think there are two giant challenges. And I really—I know I'm a very partisan figure, but I really hope today that I can speak for a minute to my friends in the Democratic Party as well as my own colleagues, speak to the country, about these two challenges. I hope we can have a real dialogue.

One is to achieve a balanced budget by 2002. Now, I think both Democratic and Republican governors will tell you it's doable, but it's hard. I don't think it's doable in a year or two. I don't think we ought to lie to the American people. This is a huge, complicated job. Second, I think we have to find a way to truly replace the current welfare state with an opportunity society.

Let me talk very briefly about both.

First, on the balanced budget, I think we can get it done. I think the baby boomers are now old enough that we can have an honest dialogue about priorities, about resources, about what works, about what doesn't. And let me say I've already told Vice President Gore we're going to invite him—we would have invited him in December, but he had to go to Moscow—we're going to invite him up to address a Republican conference on reinventing government.

I believe there are grounds for us to talk together and work together, to have hearings together, to have task forces together, and I think if we set priorities, if we apply the principles of Edward Demming and of Peter Drucker, if we build on the Vice President's reinventing government effort, if we focus on transforming—not just cutting, not just do you want more or do you want less—are there ways to do it better? Can we learn from the private sector? Can we learn from Ford, from IBM, from Microsoft, from what General Motors has had to go through? I think on a bipartisan basis we owe it to our children and our grandchildren to get this government in order to be able to actually pay our way. I think 2002 is a reasonable time frame, and I would hope we can open a dialogue with the American people.

And I've said I think Social Security ought to be off limits, at least for the first four to six years of this process because I think it'll just destroy us if we try to bring it into the game.

But let me say about everything else, whether its Medicare or it's agricultural subsidies or it's defense or anything, that I think the greatest Democratic President of the 20th century and in my judgement the greatest president of the 20th century, said it right on March 3, 1933, when he stood in braces, as a man who had polio at a time when nobody who had that kind of disability could be anything in public life and he was President of the United States, and he stood in front of this Capitol on a rainy March day, and he said, "We have nothing to fear but fear itself."

I believe if every one of us will reach out, in that spirit, and will pledge, and I think, frankly, on a bipartisan basis, I would say to the members of the Black and Hispanic Caucus, I hope we could arrange by late spring to genuinely share districts, where you'll have a Republican who may not know a thing about your districts, agree to come for a long weekend with you, and you'll agree to go for a long weekend with them. And we begin a dialogue and an openess that is totally different than people are used to seeing in politics in America.

And I believe if we do that, we can then create a dialogue that can lead to a balanced budget....

We must replace the welfare state with an opportunity society. The balanced budget is the right thing to do, but it doesn't, in my mind, have the moral urgency of coming to grips with what's happening to the poorest Americans.

I commend to all of you Marvin Olasky's *The Tragedy of American Compassion*. Olasky goes back for 300 years and looks at what has worked in America—how we have helped people rise beyond poverty, how we have reached out to save people. And he may not have the answers but he has the right sense of where we have to go as Americans.

I—I don't believe that there is a single American who can see a news report of a 4-year-old thrown off of a public housing project in Chicago by other children and killed, and not feel that a part of your heart went. I think of my nephew in the back, Kevin. I mean how would any of us feel about our children? How can any American read about an 11-year-old buried with his teddy bear because he killed a 14-year-old and then another 14-year-old killed him and not have some sense of, my God, where has this country gone? How can we not decide that this is a moral crisis equal to segregation, equal to slavery? And how can we not insist that every day we take steps to do something?

I have seldom been more shaken than I was shortly after the election when I had breakfast with two members of the black caucus and one of them said to me, "Can you imagine what it's like to visit a first-grade class and realize that every fourth or fifth young boy in that class may be dead or in jail within 15 years, and they're your constituents and you're helpless to change it?"

And that just for some reason—I don't know why, but

maybe because I visit a lot of schools—that got through. I mean that personalized it, that made it real, not just statistics, but real people.

And then I tried to explain part of my thoughts by talking about the need for alternatives to the bureaucracy, and we got into what I think has frankly been a pretty distorted and cheap debate over orphanages. Let me say first of all, my father, who is here today, was a foster child who was adopted as a teenager. I am adopted. We have relatives who are adopted. We are not talking out of some vague, impersonal, Dickens' *Bleak House*, middle-class, intellectual model. We have lived the alternatives.

I believe when we are told that children are so lost in the city bureaucracies that there are children in Dumpsters, when we are told that there are children doomed to go to schools where 70 or 80 percent of them will not graduate, when we're told of public housing projects that are so dangerous that if any private sector ran them, they would be put in jail, and we're given, "Well, we'll study it. We'll get around to it." My only point is: We can find ways immediately to do things better and to reach out and to break through the bureaucracy and to give every young American child a better chance....

I want to commend to every member of both sides to look carefully. I would say to those Republicans who believe in total privatization, you can't believe in the Good Samaritan, and explain that as long as business is making money, we can walk by a fellow American who's hurt, and not do something.

And I would say to my friends on the left who believe there's never been a government program that wasn't worth keeping, you can't look at some of the results we now have and not want to reach out to the humans, and forget the bureaucracies. And if we could build that attitude on both sides of this aisle, we would be an amazingly different place. And the country would begin to be a different place.

You know, we have to create a partnership, we have to reach out to the American people....

Our challenge shouldn't be to balance the budget, to pass the Contract. Our challenge shouldn't be anything that's just legislative. We're supposed to—each one of us—be leaders. I think our challenge has to be to set as our goal—and maybe—and we're not going to get here in two years. But this ought to be the goal. That we go home and we tell people we believe it. That there will be a Monday morning when, for the entire weekend, not a single child was killed anywhere in America; that there'd be a Monday morning when every child in the country went to a school that they and their parents thought prepared them as citizens and prepared them to compete in the world market; that there'd be a Monday morning when it was easy to find a job or create a job and your own Government didn't punish you if you tried.

We shouldn't be happy just with the language of politicians and the language of legislation. We should insist that our success for America is felt in the neighborhoods, in the communities, is felt by real people living real lives who can say, Yeah, we're safer; we're healthier; we're better-educated; America succeeds.

This morning's closing hymn at the prayer service was the "Battle Hymn of the Republic." It's hard to be in this building and look down past Grant to the Lincoln Memorial and not realize how painful and how difficult that battle hymn is. The key phrase is "As He died to make men holy, let us live to make men free." It's not just political freedom, although I agree with everything Congressman Gephardt said earlier.

If you can't afford to leave the public housing project, you're not free. If you don't know how to find a job and don't know how to create a job, you're not free. If you can't find a place that will educate you, you're not free. If you're afraid to walk to the store because you could get killed, you're not free.

And so as all of us in the coming months sing that song, "As He died to make men holy let us live to make men free," I want us to dedicate ourselves to reach out in a genuinely nonpartisan way to be honest with each other. I promise each of you that without regard to party, my door is going to be open. I will listen to each of you, I will try to work with each of you, I will put in long hours, and I guarantee that I'll listen to you first. And I'll let you get it all out before I give you my version. Because you've been patient with me today, and you've given me a chance to set the stage.

I want to close by reminding all of us of how much bigger this is than us. Beyond talking with the American people, beyond working together, I think we can only be successful if we start with our limits. I was very struck this morning by something Bill Emerson used. It's a fairly famous quote of Benjamin Franklin. At the point where the Constitutional Convention was deadlocked and people were tired, and there was a real possibility that the Convention was going to break up, and Frankin, who was quite old and had been relatively quiet, suddenly stood up. And was angry. And he said, "I have lived, sir, a long time. The longer I live, the more convincing proofs I see of this truth. That God governs in the affairs of men. And if a sparrow cannot fall to the ground without His notice, is it probable that an empire can rise without His aid?"

At that point the Constitutional Convention stopped. They took a day off for fasting and prayer. And then, having stopped and come together, they went back and solved the great question of large and small states, and they wrote the Constitution and the United States was created.

If each of us, and all I can do is pledge you for me, if each of us will reach out prayerfully and try to genuinely understand the other, if we will recognize that in this building, we symbolize America writ small, that we have an obligation to talk with each other, then I think a year from now, we can look at the 104th Congress as a truly amazing institution. Without regard to party, without regard to ideology we can say here, America comes to work. And here, we're preparing for those children a better future.

Thank you, good luck, and God bless you.

Carter, Stephen L. *The Culture of Disbelief*. New York: Basic Books, 1993.

Collier, Peter and David Horowitz. *Destructive Generation, Second Thoughts about the Sixties*. New York: Summit Books, 1989.

Dionne, E. J., Jr. *Why America Hates Politics*. New York: Simon and Schuster, 1991.

Drucker, Peter F. *The Effective Executive*. New York: Harper Business, 1967.

Eberly, Don E. *Restoring the Good Society*. Grand Rapids, Mich.: Baker Books, 1994.

Eisenach, Jeffrey and Albert S. Hanser. *Readings in Renewing American Civilization*. New York: McGraw-Hill Inc, 1993.

Gingrich, Newt. *Window of Opportunity*. New York: Tor Books, 1984.

Kemp, Jack. *An American Renaissance*. Falls Church, Virginia: Conservative Press, Inc., 1979.

Kolb, Charles. *White House Daze*. New York: The Free Press, 1994.

Murray, Charles. *Losing Ground, American Social Policy 1950-1980*. New York: Basic Books, Inc., 1984.

Nisbet, Robert. *Conservatism: Dream and Reality*. Minneapolis: University of Minnesota Press, 1986.

Olasky, Marvin. *The Tragedy of American Compassion.* Washington, DC: Regnery Gateway, 1992.

Quayle, Dan. *Standing Firm.* New York: HarperCollins, 1994.

Reed, Ralph. *Politically Incorrect.* Dallas: Word Publishing, 1994.

Rutland, Robert A. *James Madison, The Founding Father.* Indianapolis: MacMillan Publishing Company, 1987.

Toffler, Alvin and Heidi. *The Third Wave.* New York: Bantam Books, 1980.